The Human Chain for
Divine Grace

The Human Chain for Divine Grace

LUTHERAN SERMONS FOR
EVANGELICAL OUTREACH

edited by
RONALD J. LAVIN

FORTRESS PRESS   Philadelphia

Library of Congress Cataloging in Publication Data

Main entry under title:
The Human chain for divine grace.

    1. Evangelistic sermons. 2. Lutheran Church—Sermons. 3. Sermons, American. I. Lavin, Ronald J.
BV3797.A1H85   253.7   77-15236
ISBN 0-8006-1333-3

6517K77   Printed in the United States of America   1-1333

Contents

Preface

This is a book of evangelism sermons. With one exception the sermons are by pastor-evangelists of the Lutheran Church in America. The one exception is the sermon by the President of the LCA, Robert Marshall, whose support for the cause of evangelism has been a mighty factor in enlisting pastors and laity to spread the good news of God's love through Jesus Christ.

These sermons were originally preached at pastors' conferences, synod conventions, and other worship services and gatherings. They are a part of the current Evangelical Outreach emphasis of the LCA.

The cause of evangelism goes far beyond any specific church emphasis, and the need for good preaching on evangelism themes will exist until the end of time. It is in this spirit that pastors from around the country have agreed to serve as pastor-evangelists, giving a month or more per year to the task of the evangelist. Like Timothy they are trying to "do the work of an evangelist" (2 Tim. 4:5), spreading the good news of Jesus Christ as Lord and Savior and encouraging others to do the same. The word *evangelist* has fallen into disrepute among many Christians because of the charlatans and overly zealous revivalists who devour like wolves instead of loving as shepherds. The LCA is using parish-based pastors as evangelists to lift high the banner of evangelism in the context of a congregational and pastoral setting.

In the first year of Evangelical Outreach the following pastor-evangelists served in the LCA: Dennis A. Anderson of Grand Island, Nebraska; Richard E. Boye of Southhampton, Pennsylvania; Wilton Ernst of Delta, Canada; Robert L. Hock of Winter Park, Florida; Daniel Johns of Stillwater, Minnesota; Dale L. Knudsen of Albuquerque, New Mexico; Alvin Kuhn of Alexandria, Virginia; Jerald Ramsdell of Los Angeles, California; Arthur L. Ruths of Hanover, Pennsylvania; Jerry L. Schmalenberger of Mansfield, Ohio; Harold C. Skillrud of Bloomington, Illinois; James Stephenson of Hickory,

North Carolina; William Waxenberg of Spokane, Washington; and Harvard Stephens of the Bronx, New York City.

In the second year the following pastors joined the corps of pastor-evangelists: Hugh Baumgartner, Jr. of Augusta, Georgia; Ralph Wallace of Columbia, South Carolina; Paul Werger of Bloomington, Minnesota; Paul DeFreese of Omaha, Nebraska; Gary Anderson of Houston, Texas; Elton Richards, Jr. of Reading, Pennsylvania; and Dean Maas of Kansas City, Missouri.

Evangelism means sharing the good news that Christ came to earth, shared God's love with us, suffered and died for us. Evangelism means bearing witness to what God has done for all his people throughout all the earth. Evangelism means sharing the biography of Jesus Christ in the context of our own biographies. His story intersects, changes, and enlarges our stories. Evangelism means one traveler in the wilderness sharing God's food (manna) with another traveler.

This two-year emphasis of the LCA and the American Lutheran Church helps Lutherans throughout the United States to focus on evangelism. While evangelism is not the whole of our message, it is the heart of our message. The focus on evangelism as the heart of our message must never interfere with other kinds of outreach such as social ministry and social action. Too often evangelism has been portrayed as being in competition or conflict with the social dimensions of our mission as a Christian people. Outreach means bringing people into the fellowship of the church through baptism and profession of faith in Christ as Savior and Lord. It also means reaching out in love and seeking justice for the needy. We change society by converting people to Christianity. We must also change society by seeking justice, even when that means taking unpopular stands. While outreach must be personal, it must also avoid a personalism that neglects community in favor of a "God-and-me" withdrawal from the world. While Evangelical Outreach refers specifically to evangelism, it must never be in conflict with other kinds of outreach done by Christians who are motivated by genuine Christlike love.

Lutherans need to reach out to those who are unchurched. We've had a tendency to minister almost exclusively to the Germans and Scandinavians who came over from the old country. We've had a tendency to be an ingroup. We've had a tendency not to reach out to those who are in the upper class or to those who are in the lower class, since most Lutherans in America seem to be in the middle class. We need to reach out to those who are unlike us sociologically and economically. We also need to reach out to those who are unlike us in the color of their skin.

A proper emphasis on evangelism is always inclusive rather than exclusive. This means that we reach out to people who are different from ourselves and invite them to be a part of our Christian fellowship.

Preaching is one of the ways to reach out to bring people into the inclusive fellowship of Christ. Sermons are always better heard than read, but it is our hope that these sermons will be an encouragement toward better preaching as well as an inspiration to do evangelism in our congregations.

Since this is a book of sermons, the audience is likely to be mostly pastors. However, lay leaders who are interested in evangelism will find it an enriching reading experience since they too need inspiration and ideas for doing evangelism in their own communities.

I hope that this volume will contribute to better preaching on evangelism themes among Lutheran pastors and that it will help to bring enthusiastic conviction and theologically sound content to preaching on evangelism. Too often the evangelists from the fundamentalistic denominations have been the only ones associated with the word *evangelism*. Lutherans cannot agree with many modern evangelism techniques, but that should not result in our neglecting evangelism in preaching or in practice. These sermons, in style and content, should be seen as live options for evangelical preaching in a congregational setting. People have been led to a deeper faith in Jesus Christ through the preaching of these sermons, and others may be led to this kind of faith as these sermons are more widely shared.

A word of thanks is in order to Richard Bartley, Coordinator for Evangelical Outreach in the LCA; to Kent Gilbert, Executive Director for the Division of Parish Services of the LCA; and to Robert Marshall, President of the LCA, for their clear and forthright advocacy for evangelism. These Christian gentlemen have provided the structure and given the support without which an evangelism emphasis would have been impossible.

RONALD J. LAVIN

The Human Chain for Divine Grace

ROBERT J. MARSHALL
President
Lutheran Church in America

What it says is this: "God's message is near you, on your lips and in your heart"—that is, the message of faith that we preach.

If you confess that Jesus is Lord and believe that God raised him from death, you will be saved.

For it is by our faith that we are put right with God; it is by our confession that we are saved.

The Scripture says, "Whoever believes in him will not be disappointed."

This includes everyone, because there is no difference between Jews and Gentiles; God is the same Lord of all and richly blesses all who call to him.

As the Scripture says, "Everyone who calls out to the Lord for help will be saved."

But how can they call to him for help if they have not believed? And how can they believe if they have not heard the message? And how can they hear if the message is not proclaimed?

And how can the message be proclaimed if the messengers are not sent out? As the Scripture says, "How wonderful is the coming of messengers who bring good news!"   —Romans 10:8–15 (TEV)

Whenever someone becomes a Christian, three persons are involved. You are one of those. You call upon God because you believe and you believe because you heard about Jesus Christ. But you heard because there was another person who proclaimed the message. And that person proclaimed because God had sent him. God started the whole line of communication.

Tom Paine said that government grows out of the sins of people but society grows out of their virtues. Let us make no mistake about it, the church grows out of the grace of God.

In the selection of hymns for the new hymnal one popular hymn was omitted initially because it erred about the source and nature of the church's significance. It was the hymn "Rise Up, O Men of God." Some thought the hymn had been dropped because only men were mentioned and women were slighted. That was remedied easily, however, by substituting the good New Testament word for members of the church—*saints.* The great offense came in the third stanza:

> Rise up, O men of God!
> The Church for you doth wait,
> Her strength unequal to her task;
> Rise up and make her great!

Who will say the church is unequal to its task when it has the power of God at work for it? Who will make the church greater than Christ has already done in making it his own body at work in the world? The hymn spoke as though the goal was human and earthly success rather than the fulfillment of God's work.

Another hymn puts the matter correctly. "A Mighty Fortress Is Our God" says in the second stanza:

> Did we in our own strength confide
> Our striving would be losing;
> Were not the right Man on our side,
> The Man of God's own choosing,
> Dost ask who that may be?
> Christ Jesus it is he.

We are Christians because of what God has done and continues to do. Without Christ there is no strength. Without Christ there is no church. Without Christ there is no mission.

I mention mission because after the start comes the sending. After Christ there were the missionary apostles. Without the sending of missionaries, the great life and teachings of Jesus would have been lost in oblivion like most of the lives and the religious messages in the remote corner of the Roman Empire where Christianity began. No telling what your religion would be, or what kind of life you would have, since it would be untouched by the gospel of God's love, forgiveness, and care, untouched by continual companionship in faith with the Lord, untouched by the persistent energy and gifts of his Spirit. Your life would not have the benefit of all this which belongs to salvation in Christ if it had not been for missionaries sent by Christ.

God works through a human chain, as the early church shows. In the second century, there was the great teacher Ignatius in southern France. He looked back to his teacher Polycarp in Smyrna, Asia Minor. Polycarp looked back to John of Ephesus, and John looked back to Jesus of Nazareth. The human chain has now stretched to you and me. It may have been our own parents or pastors who were missionaries to us. Now we have the privilege of being missionaries to those we know and to have a part in sending others as missionaries to those we do not know.

What if those parents had not taken us for baptism? What if they had not told us the Bible stories and encouraged us to listen to others? What if those who were sent had kept silent?

A woman who became a Christian in middle adulthood found the new faith so meaningful that she told about it frequently. Often she got the reply, "Oh, I am Christian too." On occasion she was impelled to challenge the other person, "Well then, why have you been keeping it a secret?"

All of us act sometimes as though we had been given the good news about Christ in order to keep it a secret. It is well to remember the Palm Sunday story as Luke tells it. He was the evangelist who conveyed the record that some religious people criticized the disciples for proclaiming the greatness of Christ as he entered Jerusalem. Christ replied, "If they keep quiet, the stones themselves will start shouting." The question is not whether the church is great, since it is already the body of Christ; the question is whether we will be a part of that body, a link in the human chain of missionary evangelists. In other words, the question is whether we will be such members of the church as will speak so others will have the opportunity to be a part.

There are only two kinds of people in the world: those who know God loves them and those who do not. Consequently it behooves those who know to tell those who do not.

Lutherans have a distinctive contribution to make in being evangelists. This does not mean that Lutherans are entirely different from all other Christians. Rather it means Lutherans have a distinctive combination of characteristics which give them reason to be ardent in their telling the gospel story.

First, Lutherans have a confessional response to the Bible. There are many ways to study the Bible. Lutherans join those Christians who find the Bible declaring the realities about God, his saving acts, the resulting human relationship with him in faith, and the consequent relationships in human society. Much else about the Bible is interesting, enjoyable, and debatable, but the gospel message is clear. These essentials have been caught by the ancient creeds and the Reformation confessions. We have these summaries of biblical teaching that have stood the tests of the centuries. In a time when people are asking for simple and direct statements of truth, we can say the teaching of the Bible and the church is as simple as Luther's Small Catechism—and as profound. Ours is a church that looks to the Bible in that distinctive way which expects the Bible and the whole evangelistic, missionary work of the church to awaken and strengthen the confession of faith in God and his Christ.

Second, our evangelical outreach is congregational in orientation. This means continuity in our work. We do not move into a locality for a few weeks of concentrated evangelistic effort and then move out. We are in a given location as long as there are people there who will accept our ministry. Further, a congregation is a personal fellowship. While we know the value of reaching people through radio and television, the ideal is face-to-face contact. A pastor in the flesh preaches to people he will be conversing with and working with later. He is available to minister to them in times of crisis. The community of believers is gathered about the sacraments and is a caring community where Christians learn from each other, help each other, and work together for their mutual good and the good of others. A congregation is continuous, communal, and caring.

Third, our church believes the gospel is catholic in its significance. That is, it pertains to all of life. We want to avoid any schizophrenia in a Christian's life. We struggle against a divorce between worship and daily life, church and society, witness and service.

Characteristic of the Lutheran telling of the gospel is that it is:

1. confessional in essence,
2. congregational in implementation, and
3. catholic in scope.

Having mentioned service as an important part of the Christian life, we should acknowledge that the kindly act can be related to the missionary function in several ways. People could doubt the gospel message if the person telling it did not demonstrate Christian love in attitude and act. Commitment to service lends credibility to witness. Then again, the act of service, whether giving for hunger relief or working for economic development and adjustments in economic relations to allow greater opportunity for the impoverished, can be an unspoken witness to one's Christian faith.

Yet there are limits to the connection between witness and service. If our kindly deed is done solely for the purpose of influencing a person to become Christian, something is lacking in our respect for that person's integrity. Material and earthly advantages can become a motivation for church affiliation. At best the witness to the Christian faith is implicit. It can never take the place of explicit witness.

If there is to be Christian service, there must first be Christians. And Christians develop from hearing. Some things have to happen if other things are going to happen. Witnesses must be sent to proclaim if people are to hear the gospel and believe. And people must believe before their service can be motivated by the gospel. This sequence indicates the priority for the church.

I saw that priority illustrated when a committee of the National Council of Churches was working on a statement that would call upon the federal government to make a full-employment policy a top priority. Someone suggested the church should do likewise. I said, "Impossible! God has given the church other priorities. Government can write laws, develop economic policies, and levy taxes to under-write massive programs to foster full employment, and can make these top priority. The church's top priority is to proclaim God's Word, which will include a perception of human life that indeed may favor full employment but which also does much more, such as nurturing faith in the living God."

There is much discussion of the crisis in values. There are suggestions for adjustments in social institutions. There are calls for new standards in human relationships and personal convictions and commitments. The church has reason to be concerned and involved in this discussion and effort. We would not belittle their vital importance.

But the church perceives a fuller reality. It speaks of a spiritual crisis which is both deeper and more transcendent than society's value system. The church knows there must be personal change, repentance, rebirth, a new creation. The church sees the need for the revelation of the almighty God in the Christ of the cross. The church has a distinctive word to proclaim. It has distinctive sacraments, a distinctive fellowship.

The person who is going to make the gospel clearly heard so it awakens the confession of faith might have an easier time if this could be done from the pulpit. That proclamation by the pastor is an absolutely essential aspect of evangelization. Many people will not be close enough to a pulpit, however, to hear. They will need some neighbor or someone at work or at play who will have the right word to say at the right moment. The word will be immediately pertinent to some problem or some attitude. The word will come out of our having benefited from the gospel in similar circumstances. It will be a witness as genuine as our own reliance upon Christ and our empathy with the other person's trouble or joy. That word will be a link in God's chain of human transmission for divine saving grace. What God's word has started your word can continue by his grace.

You Are Blessed, Commissioned, Empowered

DENNIS A. ANDERSON
St. Paul's Lutheran Church
Grand Island, Nebraska

I generally consider myself an average, sometimes above average nice person. I'm not too bad nor too good, not unsuccessful nor a great success, an average American, a nice person generally. C. S. Lewis, the great Christian author, asks those of us who consider ourselves generally average nice people, "If you have sound nerves, intelligence, health, and popularity, you are likely to be quite satisfied with your character as it is. 'Why drag God into it?' you may ask. You're not one of those wretched creatures who are always being tripped by sex, or bad temper . . . everyone says you're a nice chap (and between ourselves you agree with them)."

If this is true that I'm a generally nice guy, why drag God into my life? God is not satisfied to leave me as the average nice guy, good but good for nothing. I don't have to drag God into my life—he is in my life like it or not. God has come into our lives through Jesus Christ that like Jesus we might not only be good, but good for something.

This morning's Bible lessons tell us of the baptism of Jesus. They give us insight into what it means that we are baptized.

In the first place baptism means that I am blessed. Jesus' baptism was a sign of a blessing from the Father. At his baptism "a voice from heaven was heard to say: 'You are my beloved Son. On you my favor rests.'" You are baptized too. In your baptism God the Father gives you a blessing. He says to you, "You are my son. On you my favor, my love, my blessing rests." This means I'm more than a collection of protoplasm, an arrangement of cells; I'm more than an animal. I'm more than a man; I'm more than an average person, a nice guy at best. Shakespeare asks:

What is man,
If his chief good and purpose of his time
Be but to sleep and feed? a beast, no more.
Sure, he that made us with such large discourse,
Looking before and after, gave us not that capability and God-like reason
To sit in us unused.

(Hamlet, act 4, sc. 4)

God has created me and blessed me to be his son, his child. I have the ultimate blessing and gift in life. God tells me I'm good, I'm worth something. I'm a child of his. My life doesn't have to be determined by my instincts, my animal drives, limited by my environment. Jesus is the Son of God. When Jesus is my Lord I too am a child of God.

Baptism means not only that I am blessed but also, in the second place, that I am commissioned. When Jesus was baptized he was commissioned for a ministry: "He went about doing good and healing all who were oppressed by the devil." Jesus was good and good for something. You too are baptized. God baptized you for a reason, that you might become a minister, a servant, a leader in our world. God has commissioned you.

This morning I invited you to think about the reason for your existence on this planet earth. To be very blunt, too many of us have been satisfied as Christians to let the world happen to us. We are content to sit back and let someone else do the doing, the thinking, the leading, and the shaping of our world. Now the time has come for men and women baptized in Christ to happen to the world, to rise up and become leaders.

There are three traits characteristic of Christian leaders. First, Christian leaders have a purpose. In Cameron Hawley's book *The Hurricane Years* a doctor reacts to a man of about forty who had a heart attack:

I see a man who is running without a goal. He has been running all his life. He runs because it is his nature to run. Once there was an open road ahead, up the hills and down the valleys, and no valley was ever so deep it dimmed the promise of what lay over the next hill. But then he lost the way. Somewhere he took the wrong turn. Now he's off the main road. He's in the deep woods. The dark shadows are closing in. He can't see ahead. But he still runs. Unless he finds his way back to the main road he will run until he is swallowed up in the black shadows of the deep woods.

Christian leaders, workers for Jesus, don't just spend their life running. They run for a purpose. Dostoyevsky says: "Without some goal and some effort to reach it, no man can live." Jesus had a purpose: "He went about doing good and healing all." What is your purpose, beyond paying off the mortgage?

Second, Christian leaders live by principles, not "what I can get by with." A baker suspected that the farmer who was supplying his butter was giving him short weight. He carefully checked the weight for several days and his suspicions were confirmed. In anger he had the farmer hauled into court. At the trial the judge was satisfied and the baker embarrassed by the farmer's explanation. The farmer had no scales, so he used for his measure a one-pound loaf of bread bought daily from the baker who accused him. A Christian leader lives by principles, not what he thinks he can get by with.

Third, a Christian leader proclaims his faith. Jesus said, "When the Holy Spirit comes upon you, you shall be my witnesses." When I have discovered or experienced something good, I talk about it. As I read the Bible I see a Jesus who did not have to go out of his way to find people who needed to hear what he taught. They were right there in front of him. So with us. When your friendship with some one grows and that person acknowledges that life is not complete, then very naturally and simply you share, proclaim to your friend what God has done for you. A Christian leader proclaims his faith.

Jesus was baptized and commissioned for a ministry. You are commissioned for a ministry.

Baptism means in the third place that besides being blessed and commissioned I am also empowered. Jesus was baptized and empowered by the Holy Spirit. You are baptized and God is ready to empower you with his Spirit. The word *enthusiasm* means literally "to be in God." I find that when I'm satisfied to live in the world with myself as the average nice guy, good but not good for anything in particular, just letting life happen to me, I soon wear out and down. I'm living in the world without living "in God." Pretty soon, when I look at life, I see more problems than possibilities; I see more reason why things will not work than why they will. David Sarnoff of RCA once said that because of his enthusiasm he was not blinded by the worldly knowledge of his scientific technicians who told him that things wouldn't work. That is why he plowed ahead and made things work. God is ready to be with you, to empower you, when you are ready to be enthused by him rather than confused by the negative powers of the world.

Be not like the mule who stands in the center of a circle, a ring of fragrant hay. The mule is hungry. There is no wind blowing, no breeze to waft the fragrance of the hay more strongly in one direction than another. So he stands there in the middle of his opportunity, but since nothing pushes or draws him in any one direction, he remains in the center and starves to death.

God is ready to empower you; he surrounds you if you'll move in his direction.

Jesus was baptized and blessed. You are baptized and blessed. Jesus was baptized and commissioned to be a minister-leader. You are baptized and commissioned to be a Christian leader. Jesus was baptized and empowered with the Holy Spirit. You are baptized and God is ready to empower you. You're not an average person. You are a child of God.

Your Highest Calling

GARY F. ANDERSON
St. Martin's Lutheran Church
Houston, Texas

One of the biggest causes of human unhappiness is that too many people are doing a job too small. Isn't it true that we are frustrated and disappointed in ourselves when we have spent hours or days or weeks doing something only to find that it really wasn't worth doing at all? Almost every one of us has experienced the disappointment of being given an assignment or a job that simply wasn't challenging enough. From what I hear from those who have been in military service, that sort of thing happened frequently under the old draft system. Someone with a master's degree would be drafted as a buck private and wind up spending a tour of duty moving files from one drawer to another and sorting paper clips. The result of that kind of waste of talent is almost always bitterness and unhappiness. Every one of us responds to a challenge. It is through being forced to reach even a little bit beyond our grasp that we are stimulated, that we become excited, that we grow.

Yet almost every day millions of us settle for the easy way out, for the second best, for less than we can really do. No wonder there is so much job dissatisfaction. No wonder there are so many who seem to be bored or unhappy with their position in life. They have simply settled for too easy a thing.

This isn't true just about our work, our vocation, whatever it might be. It is true about life itself. Too often the goals, the purposes, the objectives we have chosen for the use of our life fall short of what they could and should be. We just don't set our sights high enough. We don't take on noble enough causes. Instead, we pick second-rate goals and join third-rate forces. Many of us today complain frequently about the lack of time and how busy we are. I wonder though if a good part of the reason for our busyness is that we have dedicated our life and our time to a whole host of minor causes, while overlooking the possibly more satisfying and fulfilling commitment. We run here, we scurry there, we dash somewhere else doing a million things, none of which add significantly to our lives or make a truly meaningful contribution to the lives of others or our world. The disease and lack of satisfaction we experience is probably an inner awareness that we aren't doing the tough thing, the big thing, the truly demanding task that really counts. The great American writer Van Wyck Brooks was perhaps speaking of many of us when he described the Boston painter Appleton: "His talent had petered out in a passion for painting pebbles, which he gave his friends to use as paperweights." So too it is with many people in our time. Their talent is wasted on third-rate enterprises.

But this is true of groups also, isn't it? Social organizations, clubs, political parties, nations, and—yes—churches can all drain away their energy on jobs that are too small. The list of clubs, for example, that started out with high purposes but through the years have short-changed their objectives is almost endless. Most of us have probably belonged or still belong to an organization that has dedicated itself to doing things that just aren't important. The tragedy is that the same thing can happen in the church. The body of Christ can wrongly commit itself to doing things that just plain don't count for much. A congregation that finds itself in a rapidly growing community with many people looking for help and asking to be ministered to, but which adopts as its goal developing bigger and better potluck dinners for its own members, has settled for less than the best. A church that exists in the middle of a declining neighborhood with many people unemployed and with large groups of restless teenagers, but which chooses as its mission the installation of new stained glass windows, has not taken the high road.

What's more, the chances are good that the members of both of those churches would sense some unhappiness, some disappointment, in their chosen tasks. The reason is simple—there just isn't enough meaning in what they are doing. The church's passion is petered out in tasks without a high purpose.

God was concerned that this not happen to the prophet Isaiah or to his people Israel. He didn't want to see them wasting their time in second-rate ventures. He didn't want them to lose their sense of mission and their high calling by devoting themselves to something without a real challenge. So it is that we hear in Isaiah chapter 49, verse 6 that God says to Isaiah: "It is too light a thing that you should be my servant to raise up the tribes of Jacob . . . I will give you as a light to the nations." Paraphrased a bit, the word which comes to Isaiah tells him that the job of being God's messenger just to the people of Israel isn't big enough for him; he can do more—he has greater talents and capabilities. "Isaiah, don't set your sights too low," is what the prophet hears. Instead of just being a prophet to Israel he is to bring God's word to all the nations, and salvation to the ends of the earth. There is something which will really challenge God's servant! There is something which will require all he has got! There is a task which will truly satisfy even the most courageous and able!

The beautiful thing is that that same call has come to each of us. God has blessed us by extending a call to us which also can inspire, challenge, and fulfill the best in us. The good news is that we don't have to settle for second-rate or third-rate goals in life because we too have been called to mission. Isaiah heard that he was to be a "light to the nations." Didn't Jesus tell us that we are "the light of the world"? "Let your light so shine before men that they may see your good works and give glory to your Father who is in heaven," Christ proclaims in the Sermon on the Mount. Now there is a job worth doing! Jesus put it another way when he said we are to be the salt of the earth. Being a salty Christian, giving flavor and meaning to the lives of others, is an unending and immensely demanding task. It has called up the greatest men and women and kept them fully satisfied in its pursuit.

Our mission in life which we receive through our faith in Christ is put yet another way by Paul in First Corinthians 1:2 when he says that in Christ Jesus we have been "called to be saints together with all those who in every place call on the name of the Lord Jesus Christ." Who of us can ever be unhappy, dissatisfied, or bored with that call, the highest call that can come, the call to be a saint? Saints are God's heroes, people who serve him nobly and valiantly. Saints are those who do not simply conform to the hatred, the violence, the cheapness of life, especially in mid-twentieth-century America, but who get out there and fight to right the wrong. With Don Quixote in the musical *Man of La Mancha*, they are "willing to march into hell for a heavenly cause." That's the call which we have, each of us here today. And it is the call to all of the people who make up Christ's church. We have a call to mission.

God doesn't want us to settle for the second or third-best as his church either. It is too light a thing for the church just to take care of its own, just as it was too light a thing for Isaiah to minister only to the people of Israel. For us at St. Martin's this means that we have a high calling to make a powerful witness to the immediate community around us, to the city of Houston, and, joining with others, even to the world. Christ asks us to look beyond our own walls to care for the needs of others and to be a light to the nations. He calls us, as we have heard and sensed, to share in easing the burden of world hunger by going the second mile in our giving. Christ calls us to work out more effective programs of reaching the thousands of people around us who live in apartments, as six of our members recently learned in a special apartment-ministry seminar. And he calls us to broaden and deepen our work with the many youth of our congregation and community who are looking to the church for guidance and help, as we hope to do through the addition of extra staff. Make no mistake about it, God's word to us provides us with a job which can inspire and motivate each of us individually and all of us together as the church. "Feed my sheep," Jesus says. "Be my witnesses to the ends of the earth," our Lord calls.

So there is no reason to feel that what you and I do is without meaning or purpose. We don't need to be involved in second-rate jobs, because God has given us the highest calling any man or woman can have. We have but to do it, to join actively in his mission. This may mean giving up some of the lesser things that we do or it may mean not being so willing to settle for the easy thing, the light thing. Each of us may need to sort out some of what we do and some of the causes we have adopted, to see what really conforms to the highest calling. But if we have done that, then we know we have received the most important mission of all, and in doing his work we will be fully satisfied. We have God's high calling.

Let's Go Fishing

HUGH BAUMGARTNER
Evangelical Lutheran Church of the Resurrection
Augusta, Georgia

"And he saith unto them, Follow me, and I will make you fishers of men." I learned recently why it was that our Lord chose fishermen to be his first evangelists.

Two members of the congregation had been after me to go fishing with them. Now if there is anything that would destroy my image, it is my fishing ability (or inability, as the case may be). After running out of acceptable excuses I finally agreed to go, and then it was that my education began. Do you have any idea how early one has to get up to go fishing? It is as though you have to sneak up on the fish before they are awake. To get up at such an hour on my day off required real commitment, which is of course a first mark of evangelism. To "go into all the world and make disciples," especially in a world not particularly interested in the good news that "God so loved them as to give his Son, that believing they might be saved" requires commitment to the Lord's will. It's not easy for people to admit that they are sinners and therefore in need of a Savior. In a do-it-yourself world, grace is not an appealing idea. You've got to be committed to keep on witnessing.

After an hour's drive, which involved buying bait and a fishing license which I had never needed before, we finally arrived—or so I thought. Actually we had only reached the place where the boat was stored between these aquatic adventures. Now we had to hitch the boat to the car and start out again for the fishing site. Akin to commitment is perseverance. You have to keep on relentlessly if you expect to catch the fish, over land and water, through mud and mire and weeds. Surely perseverance is a part of evangelism; rarely does a person respond after your first effort. I read once that a successful salesman said that his best sales were made after eight visits to his customers.

When we finally came to the large lake, a hydroelectric reservoir, then began the part requiring skill. First, how to back the car so that the boat trailer entered the ramp rather than going in the opposite direction. Then one must know just when to pull the release so as to send the boat gliding into the water rather than sticking in the mud. Then you are ready for the main attraction: fishing, provided of course you haven't forgotten to transfer the tackle, bait, lunch, life preservers, water collar, and all the luxuries of home into the boat.

The second skill is getting the slippery, wiggly bait onto the hook in such a manner that you don't send it into orbit when casting. The required skills include next the ability to cast so that the baited hook falls precisely into the midst of the waiting arms of a sunken tree, the only place fish consent to bite. The hook has to be so placed among the network of limbs that it will not snag, thereby causing you to lose hook, line, and sinker, as well as patience, one's religion, and of course that clever fish you are attempting to outwit. This is no place for a novice. In evangelism also there must be skills—how to approach a person, establish rapport, witness, be persuasive.

After a while you are ready to launch out into the depths. (By now it was about the time I would have gotten out of bed on my day off.) Assured that everything is in readiness, you touch the starter of the powerful motor which will send you rushing across the waters. I never knew that a mirrored lake could be so bumpty. After a while your back reminds you how old you've become and your seat soon reminds you of when you were a child and had had a sound spanking. This all happens, of course, provided the motor starts. I recall the last time I had been fishing that you had to pull a coiled rope to make the motor start. The only time I had ever pulled a rope so long with so little result was when trying to start my lawn mower, which I should have stayed at home and done anyway, and I would have been way ahead of the game. The difference between those old starters and the powerful automatic ones is that now when they start it is with such a thrust that you may well find yourself in the water in need of being fished out. Needless to say, if you've stuck with it this far you possess patience and endurance, both of which make for effective evangelism.

Now that you are finally underway comes the essential to fishing and evangelism, namely, faith. As you gaze across that vast expanse of water bounded by miles of uncharted shoreline, it takes faith to believe you won't get lost, that the boat won't sink or the motor stop—but the greatest venture of faith is the belief that on those acres of water you are going to be clever enough to find the spot where you will be able to drop your hook full upon the fish that has been waiting there just for your arrival. I suspect that the truth of the matter is that you take the unsuspecting fish in such total unawareness that in open-mouthed surprise he swallows the hook before realizing what has happened. Then if you don't pull the line so tight as to jerk it from his mouth or leave it so loose that he shakes it free, you may land him, provided the line doesn't break or the fish doesn't succeed in tangling it around whatever—those myriads of things that clutch at your line as soon as your bait sinks beneath the water's surface.

For nearly eight hours we traversed the waters in search of fish. It is amazing how different the apparent skimming across the waters as observed from the shore is from the real thing of bumping and banging across the swells made by the wakes of the multitude of other boats in their frantic pursuit of the denizens of the sea. We tried one end of the lake and then the other, we tried the shallows and the depths, we baked in the sun and then sought the cool shadows of the lake shore where the mosquitoes were the only things biting.

Finally it was time to wend our way homeward, traveling into the setting sun. That is, after wrestling the boat out of the water and onto the trailer again. Going proudly to show our catch to our wives, if we could only figure a way to explain how three grown, strong, supposedly intelligent men could have spent so much time and effort and money only to have four small fish to show for our day's endeavor.

The only thing I could come up with was that the bait we used must have been an inferior breed and therefore not sufficiently intelligent to persuade the fish to take our hooks.

One element I must mention in conclusion—fishing is costly. When you figure what those four fish cost us in terms of man-hours, travel, and equipment, they were rather expensive. In today's world, the work of evangelism is costly also, even when the most effective techniques are used and the best witness is made. The competition for people by the many voices that call to them, the many ventures that woo them, make it necessary for those who witness to be generous with time and talents and treasures. A good fisherman doesn't count the cost if he believes the effort will bring a worthwhile catch. The chief difference in our fishing is that you don't go forth to catch fish but people, to be the children of God, to bring them to the knowledge and experience of all the blessings God has prepared for them from the time of creation. No fish that you will ever land can bring you that kind of thrill and satisfaction. Imagine what it might be like someday to have someone say to you, "I am in the family of God because of the way God touched my life through you."

A fisherman must have commitment, perseverance, skills, patience, endurance, faith, and a generous spirit. So also must one who would witness effectively for our Lord. As a Christian you become his willing instrument for catching persons. The only lure you need is love for God. The Holy Spirit will provide both the characteristics for a fisher-man-Christian, and the catch—beyond your imagining, if you are his willing fisherman.

The Apostle Peter, who was a professional fisherman, once ended a day's work discouraged by his failure to make a catch. Then the Lord Jesus came along and said, "Peter, there are fish out there, let's go catch them." Peter replied, "Lord, I fished all day and caught no-thing, nevertheless, if you say so." He went back out and the nets were filled to the breaking point. There's no question about the multi-tudes of persons to be caught for the kingdom. If the Lord says to you, "Let's go fishing," push out into the depths, trusting him to provide the catch.

Renewal in the Church

RICHARD E. BOYE
Good Shepherd Lutheran Church
Southampton, Pennsylvania

In a familiar phrase, the Commission on Function and Structure in 1971 ranked "poor morale and diminishing membership" as *the* primary concern among clergy and lay persons in the Lutheran Church in America. This diagnosis, unfortunately, is still true. Evangelical Outreach, as you well know, is one serious attempt to help put right what is thus wrong with our beloved LCA.

What we as a collective body in Christ urgently need is church renewal. As far as I can tell, we have here the most important word being bandied about in church circles today: *renewal*—not revival, not reawakening, not reorganization, not even reformation. No! *Renewal* is the preeminent word and the crying need. It was the late Pope John XXIII who lifted this word into prominence in the sixties when he summoned Vatican II and openly declared that one major purpose of the Council was church renewal. We need that yet, and we need it badly.

It is just as important, however, for us to see that there is nothing we can do to bring about church renewal. Evangelical Outreach may help us comprehend more clearly our primary evangelistic responsibility as Christians; but important as EO is, it cannot bring about renewal in the LCA. Such will come, if it is to come at all, through the Holy Spirit. The late Franklin Clark Fry put it: "The Spirit of God, and he alone, is the author of renewal." Hear that well: The Spirit of God, and he alone, is the author of renewal.

But now, having stated my theme, let me expand it. I want to lay heavily upon your hearts two thoughts which stem from this great truth that the Spirit of God, and he alone, is the author of renewal.

28

First this: *the Lutheran Church in America will be renewed only as the Holy Spirit takes hold of us, breathes new life into us, and renews us one by one.* One by one—it has to be that way. "I will put my Spirit within you," saith the Lord, "and you shall live." But you see, if this could happen to enough of us as individuals the whole church would take on a new character of vitality and growth. Outreach would be an inevitable consequence. What we sometimes sing so thoughtlessly is nonetheless literally true: "It only takes a spark to get a fire going, and soon all those around can warm up in its glowing." Many of us are hoping and working and praying that this might happen in our LCA, but we individual Christians must first let that Spirit-sent spark catch fire within our own souls.

Our problem is that it is too easy to dodge the real issue and assume that renewal must begin with that other church member over there or with that rogue who is outside the church altogether. It is said that Lutherans will rise first on the Day of Resurrection because according to the Scriptures the dead in Christ shall rise first. We can all think of people who fit into that category. I had a woman in one of my congregations who after forty years residence in another city moved back to the town where I once served. During all those years she never forwarded a communion card, never sent a contribution, never returned for a visit, never asked for a transfer. Nonetheless, after she returned from this forty years of nothingness in Christ, she promptly informed me she was a member of the church I served. I didn't think so, but dutifully I poured over the parish register trying to find her name. I looked and looked, but I couldn't find it anywhere. When I told her this and that she was therefore no longer a member of the congregation, she became irate and indignant. In fact she was so insistent in claiming church membership that I took the then current parish register and all the old ones as well to her home. I was going to show her, I was! We put those old parish registers down on the floor very carefully, for some of them were ready to fall apart. Then we knelt together, I on my twenty-year-old knees and she on her seventy-year-old knees, and we pored over those decrepit books looking for her name. And wouldn't you know it—she found her name. I had missed it somehow. I was wrong in saying it was not there. But someone decades before had written beside her name a descriptive four-letter word: "Dead!" Well, I can't repeat what that woman said then. But

I suggest that that word *dead* was an apt description of her spiritual state. Many so-called Christians are likewise dead in Christ. We all know that, and when we think of renewal in the church we rather naturally let our thoughts drift to such persons as these and then stop.

That's easy. What is not easy to understand is that if renewal is to come at all it must begin with each of us as the Spirit reaches us one by one. I can go further, and I will—though some of you might not like to hear it—and say to you that so often the trouble with the church is the trouble with us. Bite your tongue if you must, but I beg of you, do not deny the truth of that statement: The trouble with the church is so very often the trouble with us.

I am privileged to serve a congregation which has grown rather used to my strange habits, one of which is deliberately jogging in an outfit of clashing colors: red and orange. I might add that even the local dogs have grown accustomed to this eccentricity and bark their greeting as I pass by. Usually after I jog in the summer, I sit in my yard, drink my favorite beverage, iced tea, and read books. One recent summer under these circumstances I was comfortably reading a biography of the Swiss physician and healer of souls, Paul Tournier, when one sentence just about jolted me out of my lawn chair. Dr. Tournier, wrote his biographer, "began to feel that he was in greater need of religious renewal . . . than the church." Ridiculous, I thought. I knew that Dr. Tournier was a son of the parsonage, no less, and that he was no stranger in the Christian church. Moreover, he was ever ready to defend the creeds of Christendom and knew how to do it. He was also a Christian doctor. Further, he was associated with a group of laypeople and ministers who at the time were conscientiously seeking "to discover ways to revive a church that seemed to be backward and unattractive to youth." Anybody who knew him would have called him a fine Christian, but one thing of primary importance the good doctor himself conceded he lacked was a vital and personal Christian experience. The trouble with the church, he realized, was the trouble with himself multiplied millions of times over. So writes Monroe Peaston perceptively, Dr. Tournier "began to feel that he was in greater need of religious renewal . . . than the church."

This experience is the same as that of which Pat Boone writes in his autobiography *A New Song*. Raised in the church from a little boy on up, able to quote the Scriptures easily, a regular participant in family devotions, one who even preached in churches and considered himself "several cuts above the normal church member," Pat Boone nonetheless finally realized he was missing something very important indeed, and that was a firsthand experience with the Lord of the church. Then, through a series of circumstances which he fully describes in this humbly and honestly written autobiography, the Holy Spirit broke through into his life and everything became different. "The trouble was," he concluded, "I'd lived in God's house twenty-one years without meeting my landlord! I knew a lot about him—but now I've met him. I've discovered that Jesus Christ is as alive today as he was two thousand years ago when he walked the dusty roads of Galilee. And man, when you experience his living presence, not just intellectually but in your very spirit—you know it. And so my life has changed."

If this kind of experience could happen to enough of us if we would only cease our stubborn struggling against the Holy Spirit, if we were really willing to sincerely pray "Spirit of God, descend upon my heart," if we would only let the living Christ take over our lives and reign; if, in short, we would let ourselves be renewed by the Spirit, then the church we love would be swept through and through with renewal and growth. Inevitably, evangelical outreach would then take place. "Ever ask yourself why the first-century church inflamed the whole world in just a few years?" asks Pat Boone in his autobiography. Then he answers his own question: "I'll tell you why. Folks were going from house to house saying, 'Wow, something's happened to me! I've got to tell you. I've just found out about Jesus, and he lives!'"

Church renewal may start small with us as individuals, but there is a cumulative effect set into motion thereby. One plus one plus one plus one plus one will begin to gather strength and gain momentum until the Spirit of Christ, if we will but let him, will bring about renewal of the whole church in our time.

Several years ago we visited Denmark to see where my ancestors came from. One day while there we visited Kronborg Castle in the Danish town of Elsinore. This castle is famed as the scene of Shakespeare's tragedy *Hamlet*. That particular day it was the third castle we had seen, and while it is not quite true that when you have seen one castle you have seen them all, we did skip everything else there except the tour of the dungeon. I had wanted to see the chapel where my Dad told me at the end of each pew there is a carved image of the devil, symbolic of the fact that the devil also goes to church. When we built a new church in Southampton I wanted to put such an image of the devil somewhere in an inconspicuous place for the same reason, but I was voted down by the committee. They wanted more sanctified imagery in the windows and on the ecclesiastical furnishings. Even so I know in my heart that the devil still comes to my church! Anyway, that dungeon at Kronborg was both interesting and scary, but by far the most fascinating thing we saw there was the valiant Viking statue of Holger the Dane, Holger Danske, who is the Danish Uncle Sam. Of all places they might have placed that statue in Denmark, there he sits in a dimly lit dungeon, sword in hand, shield beside him, and helmet upon his head. Not only does the location of the statue raise questions, but worse yet, Holger Danske sits in that dungeon sound asleep with his beard grown round the table. Have you ever seen the statue of a hero who is asleep? Legend has it, however, that whenever Denmark is in trouble, Holger Danske, Holger the Dane, rises up, tears his beard from the table, and goes to the aid of his country.

Hold on to that a minute and let me tell you now about the most beautiful place we saw in all Denmark. It was a cemetery in Copenhagen called "The Memorial Park." The cemetery is a memorial to honor the thousands of Danish men and women who gave their lives fighting the enemy during the German occupation of Denmark during World War II. In that sanctified and beautifully landscaped ground lie the graves of 158 patriots. There are also plaques along a long wall to honor many others who "gave the last full measure of devotion" in the fight for freedom. Those thus commemorated are but a small fraction of the Danes who were killed in such tasks as taking Jews safely to Sweden in small boats, saving Allied airmen shot down over Denmark, sabotaging Nazi war materials, and spying on the Nazis and transmitting secret messages to London. Not a few were executed for such things. My own cousin was shot to death by a Nazi firing squad right there where that cemetery now stands, and his body is buried among those honored dead. When you know the story of the Danish resistance to the Nazi yoke in World War II and of those great patriots who gave their lives in this cause of freedom, you will understand why the cemetery was dedicated with the sacred words from the Old Testament: "Put off your shoes from your feet, for the place on which you are standing is holy ground." And you will understand too the words inscribed there of the pastor-poet Kai Munk, who was also martyred by the Nazis:

> Lads, you lads who died,
> You lit for Denmark
> In her darkest gloom
> A brightening dawn.

My friends, the name of Holger Danske is all over that cemetery! On the plaques, on the graves, inscribed in raised letters of bronze, carved in stone, again and again alongside the names of those fallen heroes: Holger Danske, Holger Danske, Holger Danske. That sleeping Viking did indeed rise up in a grave hour, tear his beard loose from the table where it had grown, and enter into countless individuals who would let him, who in turn themselves rose up until all together they did make a profound difference in the history of Denmark, to bring into being that little land's finest hour.

In like manner do we here—all of us—need to open our lives fully to the inrush of the Holy Spirit, to fall down in uttermost surrender to Jesus Christ as Savior and Lord, and to rise up to serve the living God. Thus renewed by the Holy Spirit shall we be his instruments in this perilous time of "poor morale and diminishing membership" to bring about the church's finest hour.

That's the first point—the Lutheran Church in America will be renewed only as the Holy Spirit takes hold of us, breathes new life into us, and renews us one by one. The second point, which is not unrelated, is this: the Lutheran Church in America will be renewed only as the Holy Spirit takes hold of us and enables us to reaffirm the power of the gospel of Jesus Christ. You see, we need to reaffirm the power of the gospel. "I am not ashamed of the gospel," said Paul to the Romans, "it is the power of God for salvation." Again, to the Corinthians, the Apostle wrote: "It is no weak Christ you have to do with, but a Christ of power." What I want to say to you now, therefore, is that the Lutheran Church in America will be renewed only as the Holy Spirit takes hold of us and enables us to reaffirm the power of the gospel of Jesus Christ.

I submit to you that we have forgotten that, or neglected it, or pushed it aside, or covered it up with our incessant busyness. The gospel is filled to overflowing with power, but we proclaim it so meekly. Here is one reason, I think, for the "poor morale and diminishing membership'' in our LCA. We are so tragically timid about declaring God's power from our pulpits and so terribly tongue-tied in trying to tell others this truth. Why? What we are needing so desperately is to have the Spirit enter in to us and reaffirm through the totality of our being the power of the gospel of Jesus Christ. Did you really hear what Paul wrote? Listen again: ''I am not ashamed of the gospel: it is the power of God for salvation.'' And, ''It is no weak Christ you have to do with, but a Christ of power.''

Underscore this fact: Our Christ is strong to save. He is fully able to help us amid the failures and perplexities and complications and heartaches and hurts that face us all in a world like this. It is wrong, I say, to keep such glad tidings to ourselves. It is wrong to be timid in sharing such good news with our brothers and sisters in human flesh. But we will become evangelists more naturally if we can come to have more buoyant confidence in the gospel's power.

The gospel of Jesus Christ is so powerfully relevant because it reaches people precisely where they are hurting. There are people both outside and inside the church who are hurting so badly; and Christ alone has the power to heal the hurts of life and to bring salvation. And where is it hurting?

People are hurting with sin. A soldier dying on the battlefield when offered medical help replied, ''It ain't such help that I want. I am a dreadful wicked man.'' Thank God there was a nurse there to read him John 3:16. Why, even the saints in the church who often stumble and stagger and fall into sin need the reassurance of how far God's love reaches. Remember, Jesus said: ''My grace is sufficient for you.'' ''Sufficient for you''—there is power in that!

People are also hurting with loneliness. A letter appeared in ''Dear Abby'' from a woman who lived in a high-rise apartment who had plenty of friends herself and therefore didn't want to be disturbed by anybody else. One evening a widow with whom she had only a passing acquaintance came to her apartment and knocked on the door. The widow said she was just lonely and wanted to visit a bit, but the other woman rebuffed her through a slightly opened door. The next day that widow committed suicide. I don't want to oversimplify a tragedy like that, but it is still true that ''One there is above all others,/Well deserves the name of Friend,'' for Jesus said: ''Lo, I am with you always.'' ''I am with you''—there is power in that!

People are hurting with all sorts of troubles. In our congregation there is an attractive former cheerleader who married the handsome football player. For many reasons they would be on top of the world except for the fact that their fine son is a hemophiliac, which has caused these parents, who love that fine lad so deeply, much heartache and emotional drain. This mother said once to my wife, "I've come to the conclusion that life is just plain hard." But we can take heart, for Jesus said: "Let not your hearts be troubled; believe in God, believe also in me." "Believe in God"—there is power in that!

People are hurting too because of the tears that come with death. I sat one afternoon for three hours in a funeral home with the family of a young, recently married soldier who was killed in Vietnam. Scarcely a word was spoken, but no one could count the tears. Another time a splendid church councilman died in the prime of life, and his body lay in state all night long in our new nave he worked so hard to build. Two times during that night the young widow called me to meet her at the church and she threw herself across that casket and cried her heart out. Who can begin to measure such grief; but Jesus said: "I am the resurrection and the life; he who believes in me, though he die, yet shall he live, and whoever lives and believes in me shall never die." "Shall never die"—there is power in that!

James S. Stewart in inimitable and eloquent words wrote:

> The constant watchword in the New Testament is not "We are able": what you do find over and over again is "He is able"—and when they say it, they are looking away from themselves to God. They are looking straight at Christ. And on this basis they proceed to make the most staggering claims. A thousand difficulties may lie across the path: he is able to bring us through! Hot, passionate temptations may threaten wreck and ruin: he is able to give the victory! The whole world may seem to be going to the devil, the human race careening headlong to destruction: he is able to bring it to God! All the way through there keeps breaking out the rallying trumpet note. He is able!

He is able! What we cannot, you see, our Lord Christ can!

Ere we finish I want to throw into the most striking contrast I can the weakness of man on the one hand and with the power of God on the other hand. What we cannot do in and of ourselves, the eternal God can and will do for us. And that is really good news. If enough of us could really believe this all the way into the marrow of our souls, we could win the whole world for Christ in this generation.

I've already told you about my side of the family, how we descended from the Vikings who, in reality, were mostly cutthroats and robbers; but my wife's side of the family, as anyone can tell by looking, is the holy side of the house. Her family is full of clergymen. There is "collar-power" all over—her grandfather, her father, her brothers, her uncles, her cousins, with even a few in-laws tossed in.

Let me tell you in particular about one of my wife's brothers, my brother in the ministry, in reality my brother. He was the secondborn of seven children in the family and, as expected, opted to become a Lutheran pastor. I'm proud to say I participated in his ordination service. In the Laying on of Hands in the ordination service this very hand, which you see before you, was placed upon his head. He was the first one I ever helped to ordain, and that service was unforgettable. As brothers in the Lutheran church, we shared with one another, preached free sermons in each other's churches, officiated together at my daughter's wedding, and talked with one another many, many times about the theological and practical affairs of church life.

Besides all this, we always enjoyed good times together. One summer during vacation from seminary, he served a church near mine and we spent at least one day a week together playing golf, swimming, and enjoying many laughs. Everywhere we have both lived we have shared vacations together and had fun playing games, watching games, eating overmuch, sightseeing, and splashing in the surf. After my wife's brother, my brother in the ministry, my brother had served in his first parish, he became a student for the Ph.D. at Duke University during which time he always, along with another brother in seminary and a sister of my wife, would join us for the Christmas holidays. Since Pennsylvania was closer than his folks' home in Colorado, they all came to be with us at that time. We really enjoyed those three Christmases together, worshiping, working, eating, playing, laughing, and talking. He even preached for me three years running on the First Sunday after Christmas, that great festival in the church year otherwise known as "The Festival of the Assistant Pastor."

Last Thanksgiving morning my dear brother, Schoneberg Setzer, received a call from the woman companion of a counselee whom he was trying to help, requesting an immediate appointment. Hoping for a breakthrough with this troubled man, Schoneberg agreed for him to come immediately to his home study even though he and his family were getting ready for church. When the man came with his woman companion, Schoneberg, as his custom was, led in prayer with his hands folded upon the Bible and his eyes closed. While he was praying, this disturbed man pulled out a concealed, razor-sharp butcher knife and stabbed my brother in the chest. When Schoneberg tried to escape and struggled into the living quarters of the house calling for help and warning his family, this hostile counselee pursued him and stabbed him again and again and again. As he lay mortally wounded with even his throat slit from ear to ear, Schoneberg uttered the words: "Please help me! Please help me!" They tried so hard to help him—the family, the dumbfounded woman companion, the police, the doctors, the nurses. They put ten pints of blood into him, but he had so many holes from that butcher knife that the blood poured out faster than they could possibly put it in. They tried so hard to save his life, but they couldn't do it. They couldn't do it! And so he died.

But our Lord Christ said: "What is impossible with men is possible with God." And St. Paul said: "In all these things we are more than conquerors through him who loved us." And in the rousing Easter hymn we sing: "Our Christ has brought us over,/With hymns of victory." And as we stood at the funeral with more poignant meaning than ever before:

> The body they may kill:
> God's truth abideth still,
> His kingdom is forever.

There is healing and saving and victorious power in the gospel, and we are called upon to be witnesses to the fact that, when we cannot, Christ is able! Christ is able! Therein "is the power of God for salvation." How dare we keep these triumphant good tidings to ourselves? How dare we?

Sharing God's Good News

WILTON D. ERNST
Benediction Lutheran Church
Delta, British Columbia

The Book of Jonah has always been a controversial book. People have struggled over whether it is the story of a real happening or whether it is a fanciful story to illustrate a spiritual message. Did the whale swallow Jonah? Or Jonah swallow the whale? Or is it just a whale of a good story?

I don't know. But what I do know is that it is a superb example of Evangelical Outreach; of a God of love, mercy, and tenderness; of a man who is self-centered, narrow-minded, bigoted; and of how God led Jonah—and leads us—to find a new and better way to share God's good news.

Three simple but mind-expanding truths shine forth from the four chapters of the book. The first is God's marvelous care for outsiders too. Jonah knew this with his intellect, as he admits in 4:2: "For I knew that thou art a gracious God and merciful, slow to anger, and abounding in steadfast love, and repentest of evil." With his intellect yes, but not with his heart! He is not ready to acknowledge that God loves the heathen Ninevites too. He loves the Jews, yes. They are his chosen people. But not those "others." And so when God said "Go and preach to Nineveh," Jonah runs the other way. Instead of going east he finds a ship going west. But of course one cannot really run away from God. And the ship tossed by wind and wave is no safe place. Jonah is thrown overboard. A great sea animal (the Hebrew word *dag* means great fish or sea animal, not necessarily whale) gulps him down and keeps him for three days and nights. Then at God's command it regurgitates him, coughs him up, and Jonah pops out like a champagne cork. And there is God waiting: "Now will you go?"

We are often like Jonah. We take care of our own—usually. But often we have blind spots in our sense of responsibility. We'd rather not be bothered with outsiders. We tend to write them off, especially if they are of a different race or color or social background or life-style. Sometimes we tend to forget the older ones or the younger ones. But God keeps saying to us, "But I love them too! And they have hurts just like you do, and they need my love and yours."

People have hurts. Many are hurting in their marriages. Sharp little digs and innuendos and one-upmanship has replaced love and tenderness and appreciation. Parents are often hurting with their children who get involved with bad companions, with alcohol, drugs, and other destructive experimentations. Young people are sometimes hurting too because their parents are too busy to listen to them, to share time with them, to help them interpret the bewilderments of growing up. People are hurting with job insecurity, with sudden illness, with growing old, with emotional exhaustion, with spiritual poverty.

I think of a doctor to whom I tried to minister whose beautiful young wife was dying of leukemia—of his long, lonely, night drives in an attempt to keep his sanity and find some meaning in God's overriding plan. Or of a businessman whom I met by chance whose conscience was heavily burdened by some earlier sin—I tried to reassure him of God's total forgiveness to everyone who asks for it, and his reply: "If I could only believe that."

We cannot resolve these hurts. We can alleviate them somewhat just by listening patiently. Most of all we can refer them to the one who can help, to the Great Healer, the Savior, the Lord of life, the God who cares, who is "able to save to the uttermost," the God who "loved the world so much that He gave his only Son" (John 3:16).

God cares for these "others" too, and he lifts our vision to see as he raised Jonah's eyes to see—and hopefully, to care.

The second great truth for me in the story of Jonah is the power of a layman's words. Jonah was a layman. There is nothing to indicate that Jonah was a professional, a theologically trained man, an ordained person, a preacher. No, Jonah was a layman whom God sent to speak to Nineveh, a big city to the east, of perhaps a million citizens, a worldly city, a wicked city. And Jonah went reluctantly.

But Jonah had fantastic results. In 3:5-10 we learn of the repentance that gripped people and king, and of the king's hope that "God may yet repent and turn from his fierce anger, so that we perish not." And God did heed their humble prayer, turned away his anger, and accepted their penitence with forgiveness. Astounding! What God could do through one layman—and a reluctant and grumpy one at that!

Evangelical Outreach has as one of its central emphases the mighty potential of the laypeople of the church. Its aim is to help build the confidence and skill in men, women, and youth of the pews to witness and to share God's good news. It's urgently needed. We haven't done so well with this in the past: there has been far too much reliance on the pastor to speak for Christ. We Lutherans have probably not done as well in this as some other churches.

I recall a time when I went into our local bank to cash a check. As the young teller looked at my name she asked, "Where is your church?" I told her. She replied, "I'm a Baptist myself. In fact I'm a new Christian. I find it very exciting."

What a marvelous little spontaneous testimony. Exciting! How often we forget the exciting challenge of being God's child, of being privileged to share our faith and our Lord with another.

Yet it is being done in our churches too. A member of our congregation who is a geologist, a scientific man and one devoted to his Lord, was doing business with a man from Japan. Somewhere in the conversation the matter came up as to how they had spent the previous day, which was Sunday. Our man said he had spent part of it in church. The other was interested. "Are you a Christian, a church member?"

"Yes, I am," was the reply, "and I find much meaning in my church and in Christ. Have you ever read his story?" The Japanese business man said he hadn't read it. Whereupon the member secured a copy of the New Testament in the Good News edition and gave it to him. Sometime later he asked his Japanese friend if he had read it. The reply: "My wife and I have read it all the way through."

People are interested today not primarily in what is written in a book, but in what is written in our lives as we profess faith in Christ. And what we have to share may be highly dramatic—like the murderer who is converted in his cell, the alcoholic who finds a new beginning through Christ, the self-hater who finds acceptance in God, the wayward teenager who finds new meaning in Christ. The dramatic, sensational entrance of God into lives like these makes a remarkable story of God's saving power. Such entrances do happen. But for most of us Christ comes more often in quiet touches, in gentle ways. Sometimes we haven't realized his closeness until we reflected on it later.

I think of my own experience—born in a humble home in Nova Scotia; baptized as a little child in that marvelous sacrament in which God accepted me as his child forever; fed on the Word at home as well as in Sunday school, confirmation class, and public worship. There were no flashing lights, no dramatic turnarounds. Just the quiet touches of his love. Like when my father was deathly sick when I was a little boy and we all prayed—I remember still going out into the barn to pray—and how graciously God spared him for many more years. Or I think of a visiting pastor who came over to me after the service, when I was in my middle teens, and asked my name and invited me to consider the ministry as my life work. God was there. God was at work, and I realized it only later.

Just so Evangelical Outreach encourages you to reflect on your own life and identify, the places where Christ touched your life in a special way, so you can share with another what your Lord and your faith mean to you.

Jonah shares, timidly and reluctantly, and the words of a layman bring renewal to the heart of a great city.

The third significant insight I find in this story is what great things God can do through our simple words. It wasn't Jonah who converted the city. It was God who used the simple words of Jonah. The people of Nineveh heard the warning. They repented. They sought God's forgiveness. God accepted them and turned away the punishment. They found life in their new relationship to God. He was their God too. He cared. Personally.

Personal care always makes a difference. I was talking to an Alberta chicken farmer a few months ago. He had twelve thousand chicks which were scheduled to be ready for the market in four months. His farm was completely automated so that for food and drink and care he would never have had to enter the chicken barn. "But I go," he said, "because I find that if I go in among the chickens and show them my interest they grow better and faster and heavier." I expressed my skepticism. "It's true," he said, "we have proved it ourselves."

If personal caring means that much to chickens, what can it mean to people! God does use our words and our concern to help accomplish his saving purpose.

A young woman was seated beside me on a flight from Chicago to Seattle. In the course of casual conversation, she mentioned that she was a nurse, twenty-one years of age, moving from Albany to Seattle to work in a cancer clinic there. She readily shared her story and I listened. Born a Roman Catholic, she had rejected both the dogmas and the church. She had dabbled in yoga, in meditation, in out-of-the-body experiences. But nothing had really satisfied her. "I'm still searching," she said. Then she asked me, "What do you think of God? How do you experience him?" And so, having listened, I had the privilege of sharing what Jesus and the church and the sacraments mean to me. "I'll think it over," she said, "and I may call you."

We plant the seed. Only God can make it grow. And he does when we share his story. That's why the Bible Study/Witness program is so helpful in our churches. It gives us an overview of God's Word with insight into the central threads of his story; then it gives us a learning experience in the process of sharing our story with the story of another and with Christ's story in a way that makes Christian sense. It is no cut-and-dried, canned program, but a living way to share our Christian experience and our personal caring so God can use it to bring forth his miracle of new life. And then through the church—the worship celebration, the ongoing Bible study, the fellowship, and the sacraments—he brings growth and maturity.

Jonah's message is as contemporary as it is timeless. It is the call of God to share his loving concern with those beyond our immediate circle; it is the inspiration of the effective layman with the Word of God in his heart and on his lips; it is the eternal promise that where his Word is shared his grace will bring new life and new power to everyone who will respond. God will keep his promises. But will we be willing to share his good news, or will we try to run away from God's challenge? He awaits our answer!

Witnesses All

ROBERT L. HOCK
St. John's Lutheran Church
Winter Park, Florida

It happened a few weeks ago on the final leg of a flying trip at the end of a long week. I was doing my homework for the next meeting in a town in Georgia, my trusty yellow pad in hand, trying to scribble down some notes for a presentation I had to make. Conditions were far from being conducive! The guy jammed into the seat next to me was smoking a cigar, one which he obviously smuggled out of Cuba during the Bay of Pigs. The teenager behind me was poking me in "areas unmentionable" with his feet. The lady directly in front had her reclining chair in bedtime position. Suddenly, amidst my frustration, a stewardess appeared like an angel from heaven. And she asked, "Would you like a drink, sir?" "Would I like a drink—Wow! But just orange juice, please. You see, I've got a presentation to make and besides I'm from the Florida citrus area, and then, too, I plan to use this whole stupid situation in a sermon up at Massanetta a few weeks from now. So just orange juice, please!" She graciously complied and began to pour some of Florida's best. But as she reached across to hand it to me, at the same time the guy next to me blew a hunk of recycled Havana in my face, the pilot hit a tremendous bump in the road, and the stewardess dropped the whole cotton-pickin' glass right in my lap! I'll tell you, there was orange juice everywhere! All over my yellow pad, my shirt and tie, my britches, even down into my shoes and socks!

Embarrassed, and with many apologies, the stewardess and my friend with the stogie both started mopping me up, using cocktail napkins which left nice little white paper lint particles embedded in my sopping wet pants. What a mess! I was a living commercial for the

Florida Chamber of Commerce. In fact I was one up on Anita Bryant, for I even *smelled* like an orange tree! (And I sure wasn't very gay!)

So that's the way my week went. How about yours? What kind of week have you had? Isn't it true we could all tell our own orange juice story? For we all have our frustrations and conflicts and uptight moments. And often over things a lot more serious and complex than spilled orange juice. We all have disappointments; we all get down and depressed and out of sorts. Indeed, some folks get so down about the world scene or their own situation that they sing that old song (with Peggy Lee) and ask: "Is that all there is? All there is to life?"

But then I saw him. He'd probably been looking at me for quite a while there in that plane. Maybe throughout the whole ordeal when I got so thoroughly juiced! He was just a little guy, maybe twelve to fifteen months old, curly hair, fat cheeks, pug nose. But he was looking at me through the crack of the seat, smiling at the frenzy we big folks were enduring, especially smiling at that poor stewardess still trying desperately to dry me off with her stupid cocktail napkins. He had a real twinkle in his eyes, and no wonder! There he was all cuddled up in his daddy's arms, a big comforting thumb in his mouth, a "Linus blanket" in his hands, completely at ease, relaxed, at peace with his world, even a world of confusion and frustration, a world of screaming jets and flying orange juice. He was grinning at me now like a kid watching the "Three Stooges." He saw great humor in the scene. And it was as if he were saying to me, "You fat, grown-up dummy! It serves you right! For that's what you get when you let yourself get all worn-out and uptight! That's what happens when you take yourself too seriously. Don't you know how to let your "Father" carry your burdens, comfort you, and enfold you with his love?"

That, you see, to a large degree, is pretty much the message Christ gave to his disciples, isn't it? The message that we who are his church have to proclaim to all people in his name. The message of our exciting new Evangelical Outreach emphasis in our Lutheran churches. The message of hope. The good news that declares: "Peace on earth; My peace I give to you; let not your hearts be troubled, neither let them be afraid. Your Father who loves you so much, who so loves the world that he sent his only begotten Son that we should not perish but have everlasting life—We are his, in Christ, we are his. He would enfold us with his love and then send us out to be witnesses all!"

But now let's be very clear what we mean by *witnessing* or *evange-*

lism. Believe me, it means very different things in this day and age. To answer negatively, here are some things from our perspective as Lutherans that we feel witnessing or evangelism is *not.* It's not the "Are you saved, brother?" approach that we hear all around us! Nor is it just another statistic we rack up with a telephone campaign in our community, because we believe people are not just statistics and are indeed tired of being just "social security numbers," or holes in an IBM card. And we believe evangelism concerns people, not numbers at all.

Nor is evangelism just getting more members to extend or save the church organization, to make our local church be just a little bit bigger and better than "St. Gertrude down by the K-Mart." So often we Lutherans seem to translate evangelism as the mandate: "Go get 'em pastor, 'cause if you don't we won't be able to float the church mortgage or pay your salary or fulfill our covenant with the synod!" Evangelism to a Lutheran is not any form of this "grab 'em and put 'em in the pew" philosophy!

Nor is it the propagation of fear tactics that so many have called the gospel! It's not some sort of a "Santa Claus religion" that says: "Better watch out, better not pout" for "God's gonna get you if you don't watch out!" That's not the kind of God Christ reveals, so such a witness is not evangelism at all.

What then really is evangelism? In the congregational handbook for Evangelical Outreach by Ray May, you'll find several definitions. William Temple said: "Evangelism is winning people to acknowledge Christ as their Savior and King, so that they give themselves to his service in the fellowship of the church." Or the definition given by the United Church of Christ: "Evangelism is getting the good news out so that people will be turned around." Or maybe you'll remember the old definition we learned years ago that goes: "Evangelism is one beggar telling another where to find food!" Indeed, the food is the very Bread of Life who is Christ himself.

Kent Knutson in a great sermon once described evangelism as "communicating the whole gospel (the love and grace of God) to the whole man!" Austin Shell in our Word and Witness books calls it a form of pastoral care! So it's demonstrating that we are all loved in Christ, proclaiming that fact, and living it, showing that we care about others, have time for them, and are willing to share what Christ means to us. In another sense, "eradication of prejudice or racism is the work of the gospel and is therefore evangelism," says Knutson. Overcoming world hunger and poverty is the work of the love of Christ, and that's the gospel, and that's evangelism! Living at peace, avoiding the devastation of war is the work of the gospel and is the work of evangelism. Resettling those Vietnam refugees is evangelism. Ministering to the kids in our colleges and motivating them to serve others is evangelism. "Whatever we do in the name of Jesus and his love—whatever we do that shows we care—is the proclamation of his mercy and grace, and that's evangelism!"

So if we reach out and touch someone in love, if we treat someone as a human being in a really human way, if we help make a person feel whole, whole in the very depth of his being, if we can give him a little hope, train him to see himself truly as a child of a loving father, that's evangelism! Whatever we do to make the gospel come alive for people, that's evangelism!

Dr. Richard Hoefler of Southern Seminary said preaching should be making the gospel real for people, "so that they not only hear it proclaimed but actually experience it and live it . . . the gospel entering their lives and bringing change and making people whole and at peace and full of the joy of their salvation!" That's evangelism!

But if that's what evangelism is, and if that's what our calling as individual Christians and congregations is and has always been about, then it's not too hard to recognize that we in the Lutheran Church have a few problems to overcome.

I heard a lawyer, the mayor of Jacksonville, say recently that he used to think the only time you were supposed to witness was when you got a subpoena to appear in court! A lot of us, especially us Lutherans, still seem to believe that, and we of all people ought to be held in contempt!

Louis Almen, in his book *Evangelical Outreach Foundations* talks about this problem—about the lack of the sense of evangelism and witness in our Lutheran Churches. He reports a recent study of Lutheran attitudes and behavior in North America and says that only 44% of our Lutheran people could report engaging in any activity which could possibly be interpreted as a "witness for Christ" in the last year!

One of our youth in a Youth Convo Bible Study session put it this way: "A lot of times at school I know a friend is really hurting. He's got a big problem to work out, he needs help, and I know also as a

Christian that I have the answer he needs in Christ. The trouble is," he said, "it's just so tough to express it, to show it, and often the opportunity slips right through my fingers."

Another youth added: "Yeah, sometimes I feel like a hypocrite, singing all those hymns down at church on Sunday, praying all those prayers, and then at school not even wanting to appear to be religious, for fear someone will think I'm a freak or a square!"

We *all* know precisely what these young people mean. Christ called it "hiding our lamp under a bushel" and we *all* do it, pastor and laypeople, and we do it over and over and over again! Someone has said we Lutherans have so much awe and respect for Jesus Christ that we're afraid to even use his name in public!

So, we've got problems, and part of the Evangelical Outreach emphasis is to finally admit the fact, as hard as that is for us to do; and to try to change the attitudes and religious lifestyle of our pastors and people; to motivate us all to get rid of the barriers that prohibit real evangelism among us; and to change the climate in our hearts, in our homes, and our congregations, that we might more fully share the good news!

Let me list just a few of the problems in our church climate we hope Evangelical Outreach might help us solve together.

When the fourteen of us Lutheran Church in America pastor-evangelists met in retreat last fall, we decided to list what we felt were some of the major barriers to evangelism in our Lutheran congregations. You might be surprised that at the very top of the list we put the extremely low morale of our pastors! The depression and low spirits of our clergy, who are often overburdened and overstressed and yet equally often underaffirmed and underloved by their people.

I talked with one of our pastors and his wife at our synod convention. They shared the agony they felt when they went through a period in their ministry when their people "had a gun to their heads" and refused to express to them in any way the love of Christ! Nothing must be more painful to endure than this, and yet so many pastors are experiencing it year after year.

I ask you, how in the name of God can we expect our congregations to get all fired up about evangelism (or anything else for that matter) when so often the one called to be the "enabler," the one who should "spark the fire," has all but flickered out! He can't even "flick his bic" and yet we call on him to light the fire!

We hope Evangelical Outreach will lead us to unburden our pastors, even when they resist (and most clergy will do just that!). We must, so that the *laos* will indeed be "the people of God," be ministers, and express their love of the Shepherd of our souls. Luther, 450 years ago, reminded us of the priesthood of *all* believers . . . that we are *all* called with a holy calling to be the church, Christ's body.

A second concern revolves around how much our congregations witness simply by caring for people and showing it in the name of Christ. The best witnesses we have are those who have been touched by the love of our people, who've seen the congregation put food on their tables and pay the rent when a job was lost, or support them with love during a crisis or a bereavement. Get someone who has experienced our shouldering of his burdens and you've got a witness, and he's a witness not just to the work of the congregation that cared for him, but to the love and grace of our Lord who moved us to care and show it! Like the lady Dr. F. Eppling Reinartz quoted who said, "This is a great church because if you join it you never again have to share a burden alone."

We had a Youth Sunday a few weeks ago at St. John's, and the youth put on a little chancel drama about Christ healing the blind man and about the blindness we Christians so often show to the needs of others. Then they called upon a young man in our church who is physically blind. His name is Rick Agman and he's married to a girl who spent much of her life in a crippled children's home. I just wish you could have heard the witness to Christ this blind man made! For he said he realized more and more that his physical blindness wasn't really a handicap. That it only helped him see how spiritually blind so many people really are. He shared what he meant by telling how just a few years ago he had been healed of his spiritual blindness and through Christ had found "light in his darkness," the sight that really counts.

But then he announced something special . . . that he and his wife Joyce had just adopted a little boy, and that the little one was blind too! Imagine the courage it must have taken! He went on to say that he hoped God would lead and enable them to share the gospel with their son as the congregation had done with them. And then he added that they had decided to name their child Robert, after Pastor Bob! Not that I had done so much. I was just the symbol of how dear that church is to them and how that church has been with them through all their troubles and witnessed to the love of Christ.

But there's one more point I'd mention about our church climate that I hope Evangelical Outreach will help change. And that's the tone of our worship.

Our Youth Convo used words like "dull, boring, weak" in describing worship back home. We hope Evangelical Outreach will help us really celebrate when we gather in his name. The youth of the Florida Synod's Convention led us in worship and even asked us to dance to the Lord! God wants us to make our liturgies come alive and our sermons exciting and full of enthusiasm, maybe even a bit emotional! At Kenosha leading pastors and theologians sang, of all things, "Amazing Grace." And I was moved by the old hymn, and I wouldn't be surprised if a few of the rest of those old stick-in-the-mud Lutherans went to sleep at night with that song echoing in their ears! It moved us—and dear God, what's wrong with that when we gather to celebrate the good news?

A couple of Sundays ago we baptized that little blind baby I mentioned a few moments ago. And I preached on baptism. I got along fine at the first service, but when it came time to baptize that little blind kid named Robert, I'm telling you, we *all* wept with joy and with love! And we worshiped as we wept!

So, there's really nothing new about Evangelical Outreach. "It's a twenty-century-old concern." The purpose of it is simply to remind us who we are and whose we are; that we were chosen by him to share the gospel with others where that gospel has been experienced in our lives. It's an emphasis to remind us that we are called to be co-laborers with the Lord, as Paul put it: "ambassadors for Christ, God making his appeal through us!"

So that young blind man on Youth Sunday in our church witnessed to us; he evangelized us! That crippled old lady in your church who smiles at you when you visit her and has more for *you* than you for *her* . . . she witnesses with her joy for life and for her Lord! And that's what we are all called to do. To place ourselves at God's disposal, with the fire, the enthusiasm, and the zeal of the gospel: "That we might declare the wonderful deeds of him who has called us out of darkness unto his marvelous light."

Tell Me It Isn't So

H. ALVIN KUHN
Peace Lutheran Church
Alexandria, Virginia

When Jesus sent out the twelve disciples as the first traveling evangelists he did not provide them with a manual entitled *How to Win Converts; or, Evangelism Made Easy—Five Steps to Guaranteed Success.* The instructions he did give them, found in the first part of the tenth chapter of the Gospel According to Matthew—"Take no bag for your journey, nor two tunics, nor sandals, nor a staff . . . if any one will not receive you or listen to your words, shake off the dust from your feet as you leave that house or town"—are certainly not intended as a training course for contemporary witnesses. Indeed no part of the Bible, Old or New Testament, was written to be used un-interpreted as a chart of instructions for twentieth-century congregations. While the human situation hasn't changed a great deal, the kind of world in which we humans live has changed drastically. That is why the good news of Jesus' redemptive death and resurrection, to which the Bible bears witness, cannot be locked into just one pattern of presentation or made into one form of "doing evangelism." God and his love for his world are bigger than that.

That is also one of the reasons that Evangelical Outreach, now a part of the life and ministry of the Lutheran Church in America, is an emphasis rather than a program. We are concerned not so much with producing a set of instructions for congregational evangelism committees, but with helping each congregation develop an interest in and a climate for sharing the good news. Then, if the motivation is present, they can put together a structure that will enable the witnessing function of that congregation to be done as naturally and effectively as possible.

Central to it all of course, whatever the form or type of program that emerges, is the individual Christian's awareness of who he or she is in the sight of God. For without the conscious awareness that you and I indeed have good news—joy—to share, all evangelism becomes a duty, a burden to be borne, and usually little more than an invitation to join our "club." I need to know, not just with my head, but also with my heart—my whole being—the reality of my salvation, the reason for my hope, or I have nothing of ultimate value to share.

That came home to me in a new way a few months ago as I was driving south out of Wilmington, Delaware. The radio was on, and as I moved beyond the range of our local station I flipped across the dial to hear what Baltimore might have to offer. Purely by chance I picked up one of those stations that specialize in fifteen-minute recorded religious programs, one right after another. Since we all need to know what's happening in our field, I listened for awhile. I have no recollection of the name of the man who was speaking, but I do remember a few of the things he said. Someone had written him, complaining that his television program (he evidently used that means of communication as well as radio) was shown in her area only on Sunday mornings during the hours for church services. Why, she wanted to know, did he choose that time, when most people could not tune in? The letter writer must have been from New York City, for in his reply the evangelist said that on any given Sunday 89% of the people in New York were not in church. I don't know where he got that statistic or how accurate it is. It doesn't really matter, for it was his next sentence that really grabbed me. He continued, "And of those that are in church, 67%—that's two-thirds—don't know why they are there, don't know what it means to be saved!"

It sounded a little far-fetched and I didn't think much more about it until a short time later as I was looking through a copy of the periodical *Christianity Today*. In that particular issue there was an interview with Bill Bright, the founder and president of Campus Crusade for Christ, the group responsible for the "I Found It" campaigns in a number of our cities. Dr. Bright was asked, among other things, this question: "Can anyone in America possibly say that he or she has never heard the story of salvation?" He replied, "Our surveys —we take hundreds of them—show that about half the church members are not sure of their salvation, that 95% do not understand the ministry of the Holy Spirit, that 98% are not regularly introducing others to Christ.'' There was more to his answer, but I was struck again with this assertion—this accusation, if you will—that half the people who make up the membership of our congregations don't know what it means to be a Christian, aren't sure of their salvation. Tell me it isn't so! Tell me that you are here this morning because the living Christ does have a commanding place in your life, that you are a member of the church because you are conscious of your dependence upon the God who creates and redeems each one of us, that you are indeed sure of your salvation.

I realize of course that traditionally Lutherans often find it difficult, if not impossible, to talk about their faith with strangers or to demonstrate the joy that comes with the awareness that we are acceptable through God's forgiving mercy. But I will not concede to anyone, be he radio evangelist, or Bill Bright, or Billy Graham, or Robert Marshall, my conviction that by the grace given me in Jesus the Christ, I can stand before my God confident and unafraid. I know where my salvation lies and so do you. Not with us, but with God!

Being as fundamental as I can be (and in the very best sense of that word) let me share with you three simple facts about our salvation, a kind of three-part answer you can offer to anyone who wants to know if you are saved, if you are sure of your salvation. Look them straight in the eyes and say, Yes I am, because:

First of all, someone has shared with me the good news, the gospel, the story of God's gracious act in Jesus the Christ. Someone, be it mother, father, grandparent, teacher, friend, someone who cared about my well-being, took the time to tell me about the God they knew and loved. That's where it begins—the awareness of this thing we call salvation—with the most ordinary witness a Christian makes to another human being about the faith. It may be within the family, in a church-school class, at work, in a car pool, around a bridge table, in a hospital room, anywhere. It may be rather formal in presentation, or in the most casual of conversations, or simply a part of a daily pattern of reading the Bible and saying prayers. In whatever form it comes, it starts the process of awakening within us thoughts about who we are and who God is. It opens the way for the Holy Spirit, who always accompanies God's word, to plant the seed of faith or to nurture the growing plant. You may not know all the details of the story, like the dates of King Herod's reign or all the names of the twelve disciples—you don't need to. You do know that in that man of Nazareth God acted to restore the relationship of love and trust our sinfulness keeps breaking. You know that in the life and death and resurrection of Jesus the Messiah, the victory over sin and death was won for all people and for all time. You know that story, and that's part of your answer.

There's a second part, equally important. If someone asks you, "Are you sure of your salvation," without a moment's hesitation you can reply, "Yes, I am, because I have found in that story of Jesus the Christ a center for my life. I believe it is true, not just as historical fact, (indeed, some of the facts are very much in debate and likely will always be so) but it is true for me in a much deeper sense. It gives meaning, purpose, and direction to my daily living. It makes a difference in the way I set my priorities, in the way I reach decisions, in the way I seek to fulfill the trust committed to my keeping."

If I am sure about my bank account I use it to write checks or as collateral information. If I am sure of my salvation I use it as a rock on which to stand, as a guide for action. It gives me a perspective on history and a hope for the future. It is the most precious gift I have, and one that cannot be taken from me no matter what happens to me in this world of uncertainty and suffering. That's the second part of our answer. First, I know the story of Jesus the Christ; second, his life and death and resurrection are a vital, guiding, sustaining part of my life, my story.

There is a third part of our answer to those who have questions about our salvation. It is the answer of faith, or better, of trust or commitment. It says without reservation: Yes, I am sure of my salvation because that salvation depends not on my worthiness but on God's gift; not on my faith, but on the faithfulness of God. If I had to measure against some standard (the Ten Commandments or the Golden Rule, how much I have done, how much I have given, how well I have served) I could never be sure that the scales were tilted in my favor. Praise be to God, I don't have to depend upon my own efforts, my own goodness, for my salvation, and neither do you. It's as simple as this: Are you willing to accept, in humility and trust and with thanksgiving, God's acceptance of you? That's the only condition—our trust in his grace.

Are you sure of your salvation? Well just in case Bill Bright is doing one of his surveys in your area this week, let's change his statistics. Tell the questioner firmly, confidently, joyfully, "Yes, I'm sure, for I know the God revealed in the resurrected and living Christ, and I can depend on him!"

There Is Good News

JERRY L. SCHMALENBERGER
First English Lutheran Church
Mansfield, Ohio

The Savior said to the people around him, "The Law of Moses and the writings of the prophets were in effect up to the time of John the Baptist; since then the good news about the kingdom of God is being told."

—Luke 16:16 (TEV)

The angel announced the birth of Jesus like this: "Don't be afraid! I am here with good news for you, which will bring great joy to all the people."

—Luke 2:10 (TEV)

Today's English Version of the New Testament calls it "Good News for Modern Man." Fifty-two times the New Testament talks about the *good news.* We often mention *the gospel,* which means good news. But do we worship and live and witness to this terrific news?

I think not! Because I believe many of us forget what the news is that we bear and just how good it is! When we have great news to tell —such as the birth of a new baby, a large raise in our salary, a new and better job, an engagement, a new boyfriend or girlfriend—we literally shout it from the housetops. But not so the gospel of Christ. In fact, we are very reserved and timid about making our witness. Probably because some denominations tend to be obnoxious in witnessing, because we tend to stress "order" and being "in control," and show little emotion, and because we tend to give responsibilities like this to committees anyhow. We really cool it about the gospel and our responsibilities to share it with others.

"I reckon him a Christian indeed," wrote Matthew Henry, "that is neither ashamed of the gospel, nor a shame to it."

"We believe it in a way," said Robert Rainy of the gospel, "but we are no longer startled by it in our own minds."

I have an idea about the real reason that we forget to witness to our faith. We forget how good the news is that we have, and we have taken it for granted for so long and been so confident of it all along that the thrill and excitement has dimmed. I heard once of a little boy who had gone to Sunday school and had the pastor for his teacher. The pastor explained how God was everywhere that the little lad looked. The next day, sitting at the breakfast table, the little fellow looked up at the kitchen cupboards and asked his mother, "Is God in those kitchen cupboards?" The mother answered, "Yes, son, God is everywhere that you look, just as Pastor reminded you." Looking around the room further, the young lad pointed to the refrigerator and asked, "Is God in the refrigerator? Is he there even when the door is shut and the light is out?" The mother patiently explained that wherever the young lad looked, there was God. The boy then picked up the sugar bowl on the table, and lifting its lid just a little, peered inside and asked "Mother, is God in this sugar bowl right now?" The mother began to assure the lad that indeed God was in the sugar bowl. The little boy slammed down the lid and said, "I got him!"

Perhaps you and I often practice our Christian religion like that young lad with the sugar bowl. We try to keep the Spirit of God and the excitement of the good news contained in certain safe perimeters.

Each evening John Chancellor, David Brinkley, Barbara Walters, Harry Reasoner, Walter Cronkite all broadcast a morbid lot of details called the evening news. When so much of the news is rotten and seems to carry with it so little hope, let's you and I concentrate on the good news that we Christians have to broadcast to the world. Hughes Wagner wrote in *The Presbyterian Record*: "If a person is a socialist or a communist, I will know it in twenty-four hours; if he is a member of a labor union, I will know it within a few days; but if he is a member of a Christian church, it may be years before I will ever learn of it."

"When it comes to speaking about their faith, some folks are like rivers running into the North Sea—frozen up at the mouth," says Dick Ferrell. If indeed this is the situation in our Christian churches, then we must throw up against this information that which Halford E. Luccock claims when he says: "The church that does not reach out will fold up."

It certainly will be profitable for us to look at and renew again the facts of the good news for Christians!

God loves us. John 3:16, 17 puts it: "For God loved the world so much that he gave his only Son, so that everyone who believes in him may not die, but have eternal life. For God did not send his Son into the world to be its Judge, but to be its Savior" (TEV).

That is really good news! In a world where we see the evidence of hate in so many places—where marriages struggle and break up, where self-worth is questioned, where the races are divided, and where vengeance and getting even are top priorities—we have good news: God loves us.

To be loved is a glorious thing. It gives such a different perspective on life, and really makes us come alive. Watch teen-agers who fall in love, watch people of any age who know they are loved, and you will see a whole different kind of person and attitude towards life.

William Jennings Bryan told of a farmer boy who after months of bashfulness finally said to the girl he loved, "Mary, I been lovin' you for a long time. I can't talk much, but will you be my wife?" Mary replied, "Yes, John, I've been loving you too. I'll be happy to be your wife." Late that night when John was alone, he looked up at the stars and was heard to say, "Oh, Lord, I ain't got nothin' agin nobody now." To be loved is a glorious thing and part of the good news that we share.

So to you who are lonely, to you who doubt your value, to you who are afraid, to kids whose parents neglect them, and parents whose kids hurt them, to you who take a stand unpopular with the rest of the people, there is very excellent news. The scripture assures us: God loves us.

If you have let your picture of God dim and slip and he seems like a stern judge, a wrathful avenger of people, take heart: today there is good news. God loves you. "God did not send his Son into the world to be its Judge, but to be its Savior." "This is what love is: it is not that we have loved God, but that he loved us and sent his Son to be the means by which our sins are forgiven" (1 John 4:10).

This brings us to the second thing we believe: we have sinned. "All have sinned and come short of the glory of God" (Rom. 3:23). The temptation is to think that we are better than we are. The good news includes the fact that we are sinners, that we don't live up to the faith, that self often gets in the way of God, and that our lives are often selfish. When Amfortas drew near to the Holy Grail his flesh quivered. So, the proximity of the believer to Christ gives him a sense of his own need and sin. We need to be reminded again and again that we are sinners because the intensity with which we believe that we are imperfect and sinners is the intensity with which we feel our need for God and his forgiveness. Perhaps it is true that, because we don't feel very strongly our sinfulness, we don't feel very strongly that we have a great gift in forgiveness.

Let's renew again our insight that we do fall short, and do stray, and do desperately need God's forgiveness. Isaiah 53:6 puts it: "All we like sheep have gone astray; we have turned everyone to his own way." So we see—God loves us, we have sinned, and we may be saved. "This is a true saying, to be completely accepted and believed: Christ Jesus came into the world to save sinners" (1 Tim. 1:15).

If we have come to a desperate knowledge of our need to be saved, then here we have very good news! Jesus Christ does it. Like a woman rescued from her burning home, like a drowning child pulled from a lake, like a choking victim given breath, like a lost person being found, like a reprieve for a condemned person, we too have a rescuer, one who snatches us from death and gives back our lives. Not only does God love us, he gets involved—he jumps in and saves.

John Baillie, in his *Invitation to Pilgrimage*, writes, "Christ did not come to earth merely to tell us what to do; he came to do something for us. He came not merely to exhort, but to help. He did not come to give us good advice. There are always plenty of people who are ready with their advice. Advice is cheap, but what Christ offered us was infinitely costly. It was the power of God unto salvation."

"For the Son of man came to seek and to save the lost" (Luke 19:10).

Now comes the part of the good news that we sometimes omit: It's *now*. 2 Corinthians 6:2 says: "Now is the accepted time; behold, now is the day of salvation" (RSV). Proverbs 27:1 puts it: "Never boast about tomorrow. You don't know what will happen between now and then" (TEV). Isaiah 55:6 says: "Turn to the Lord and pray to him, *now* that he is near" (TEV).

Very much a part of the good news is its urgency. It is breathlessly told in the New Testament. It's an "extra, extra, read all about it" news. The good news we share is *now* news. It must not be delayed or put off. The water of our baptism leads us to get this news immediately to all of God's people. People are guilty; people die; people are desperate; the news about the Savior is *now*. We often hold onto the news so long, as if we had forever to tell it. But proclamation of the gospel is immediate. When someone is drowning or choking or burning, we don't wait with help—so, too, salvation is immediate and now.

The most wonderful story a person can tell is that of the difference which Christ has made in his or her life. The most gratifying satisfaction a person can experience is to share that difference with one who has lost his or her way. The sharpest dividing line cutting across our world today is the one separating those who believe that there is such a God as Christ revealed and those who do not. To bring a person across the line of faith in Jesus Christ is the basic Christian responsibility. It is the surest service to him who said, "You are my witnesses."

One more element of the good news: It says that if we neglect it we will certainly perish, but to believe it means to come alive. There is always this element in the news we tell. Scripture says: "How then, shall we escape if we pay no attention to such a great salvation?" (Hebrews 2:3, TEV) "For sin pays its wage—death" (Romans 6:23, TEV). Jesus said, "I tell you that if you do not turn from your sins, you will all die" (Luke 13:3, TEV).

Emil Brunner said: "The greatest sin of the church is that it holds the gospel from itself and from the world."

We must not leave this work up to the few faithful on a committee. Everyone is an evangelist and responsible to proclaim the news. It is so urgent and so immediate that every member of the congregation who knows the news must share the news. It is the heart of Christian responsibility.

We often skip over this element of the good news. That's the bad news for those who ignore the good news. That makes our privilege of telling it and witnessing even more urgent. Spiritual life and death are involved. We just cannot neglect the telling of the receiving of this message.

E. Paul Hovey writes:

When I began to understand what the Christian faith is and what it could mean to me, I concluded it was not mine to keep. It was something I had to share. I became interested in evangelism. To me this is both natural and necessary to living a full Christian life, for evangelism means sharing one's faith. You need not have had a startling dramatic religious experience in your life in order to share your faith. God calls each one to witness for him in a special way . . . . God is seeking to fulfill his purpose through you. To fail to share one's faith is to stand in the way of God's purposes. Realizing this, you will come to say of your faith, "It is not mine to keep."

However, the Bible not only warns us of neglect; it also promises us that if we believe, we will live!

John 5:24 says: "I tell you the truth: whoever hears my words, and believes in him who sent me, has eternal life. He will not be judged, but has already passed from death to life." John 6:37 puts it: "I will never turn away anyone who comes to me."

We are saved; we are the saved—we sinners get undeserved salvation, and that's very good news. When we believe and all this becomes real to us we begin to really come alive.

Said a guide in a picture gallery, "Every time I try to explain these pictures, I see more to explain." This is true also in matters of faith. As we seek to win others to our faith in Christ, our faith is deepened and our knowledge of Christ is increased.

To know God loves us, to be aware of our sins, to see our salvation in Christ, to recognize the urgency of our message, and to realize that we dare not neglect it is all part of the grand and glorious news. When we do all this we come alive with this glorious news that we have, and our lives are redirected and changed and inspired. We simply cannot contain ourselves, but must share the news.

The little boy that I mentioned earlier went back to his church the next Sunday and asked his pastor about God being in the sugar bowl. He told the pastor that his mother instructed him that God was bigger than a sugar bowl and that he couldn't capture him there. The pastor affirmed that that was correct. In fact, he told the little lad that God was bigger than the mountains. The young man asked the pastor, "Is God bigger than my Daddy's garage?" The pastor assured him that God is. The little boy then asked an important question for us to answer as well: "If God is bigger than my Daddy's garage, and God is inside me, why doesn't he stick out?"

Not Obligation, But Opportunity

HAROLD C. SKILLRUD
St. John Lutheran Church
Bloomington, Illinois

All visitors to our nation's capitol are treated to a colorful display. The American flag is unfurled everywhere. Colorful banners adorn the streets. Placards with messages of protest or support are visible on every hand. This is Washington.

Recently however, a Washington family named Salvatori displayed these emblems for a most unusual purpose. It was their custom to fly the American flag in front of their home daily. It was just a normal practice. Likewise, another normal practice was the morning departure of their son Billy, a sixteen-year-old sophomore in high school who, together with three of his other buddies, went by car each morning to school. On this particular day, the thirteenth of May, for some unknown reason the car went into a skid, smacked into a tree, and all four of the boys were seriously injured. Billy Salvatori suffered the worst. That morning the family, close friends, and the parish priest began a long, anxious, lonely vigil, waiting for Billy to regain consciousness. Twenty-four hours, forty-eight hours, seventy-two hours passed. Then they began to realize that this was going to be a very long, agonizing experience.

The Salvatoris were well known in their community and parish, so frequently the telephone would ring and people would ask, "We're interested in Billy. How is he doing? We are praying for Billy. Has he regained consciousness?" Soon there were too many calls for the family to cope with. So they developed a signal. To the community they announced, "We fly an American flag in front of our home daily. We're taking the flag down. Watch our home, and the moment Billy awakens from his unconscious state, we'll put that flag back in the socket. That signal will tell you that Billy's awake." Day after day friends in the neighborhood kept their eyes focused on the empty flag socket. As word spread in the city, hundreds of others joined the anxious vigil. Days passed, weeks passed, and soon it was almost a month.

Finally the day came! One morning as the people left their houses, walked down the sidewalks or rode down the streets in buses and cars, they saw what they had prayed and longed for. The flag was flying. And mounted on top of the flag was a bright, colorful, red ribbon waving in the breezes. Finally, nailed to the outside of the front door where all could see, was a huge placard: "Billy's awake! Praise the Lord!" The exciting news spread like wildfire around the entire community. "Billy's awake! Praise the Lord!" Everywhere people were sharing the good news that Billy was going to get well.

There is something spontaneous and contagious about good news. It must be shared. We don't have to look for good news. Those who have it pass it on to others. That's why the early church grew. There is no other way to explain the amazing, spontaneous growth of the early Christian church. These early Christians had also known the dreadful, anxious moments of waiting when Jesus was nailed to the cross that fateful Friday. When then they were privileged to witness his presence on Easter, they simply had to share the good news: "Jesus lives!" People responded to this witness in faith, "and the Lord added to the church day by day those who were being saved."

It's the nature of good news to be shared. And good news is good news only so long as it is shared. When it stops being shared it is no longer good news. In time the news about Billy Salvatori will cease. The time will come when no one will tell another or point to the flag and the placard on the door. It will then cease to be good news. Good news remains good news only so long as it is shared. That's true with the good news of Jesus Christ too. The reason it has come down to us through the years is because it has been shared. It remains perpetually good news by virtue of the fact that it is being shared, one person to another—told, shared, and experienced.

Now, today, we are the church. We have the opportunity to be bearers of the good news. Sometimes you and I wonder how effective we are. I was meeting sometime ago with the vice-chairman of our church council, making plans in preparation for the Evangelical Outreach emphasis in our own congregation. In the middle of our conversation he suddenly blurted out, "You know, I've got to be very honest. That hymn we sing in church sometimes, 'I Love to Tell the Story,' well, I like that hymn. I know the words from memory and I sing it heartily in church. But you know pastor, in real life I must admit I don't love to tell the story. If I am going to be perfectly honest, I am terrified with the very notion. I am not comfortable when I know that I am to share the story with others. I like the hymn, but I don't really love to tell the story." We agreed that we would check this out further and see how other members of the congregation felt. The following Sunday morning we passed out a questionnaire at the adult forum. One of the questions had to do with how we feel about sharing the good news with others. About 125 copies were returned, and when we tabulated them we discovered that practically all agreed with our vice-chairman. When people were asked on that questionnaire, "Why do you feel that way?" reports came back something like this: "Well, my faith is so personal, so private, I don't feel comfortable sharing it with someone else." Or, "I don't feel qualified to do this. Who am I to think that I can go out and bear witness to someone else? I am just an ordinary person." Or, "I don't want to be regarded by my friends and neighbors as some kind of a fanatic."

We discovered a common thread in these responses. First, there was the ready admission that the church's central task is sharing the good news of Jesus Christ. It is his commission: "Go into all the world and bring the gospel to every creature." Coupled with this was a feeling of discomfort and inadequacy. In a real sense, sharing the good news had become a burden, an oppressive task. It was seen as an obligation to be successful salesmen for Christ. And precisely therein lies the problem. We have come to look upon witnessing as a task which requires a certain kind of expertise. Like a salesman who goes out to market his product, who has to gain a thorough knowledge of the product, who has to learn skills of communication, who has to understand psychology, who needs to know how to close the deal—we may feel we must master these techniques. Not many people make good salesmen. Most who try it fail. Most of *us* would not make good salesmen. And if that's what we think we are called to do—to go out into the world and persuade people who are not presently believers to become believers in Christ by using our persuasive techniques, our arguments, our knowledge—we become terrified. But let's remind ourselves that the term "salesman of the gospel" does not appear in the New Testament. We are not called to be salespersons for Christ. Instead the New Testament calls us to be "witnesses for Christ." What a remarkable difference!

One Monday morning recently, while sitting at my desk in my study, I happened to glance out my window and saw a number of cars on the church parking lot. People were coming and going in large numbers. Since our building is used by a variety of service-oriented groups in the community, I paid little attention at first. However, as more cars came and went, I began to wonder what was happening. Then it dawned on me. This was Weight Watchers day. Now this is the one commercial group we permit to use our building because we give the net proceeds of the rental fee to the World Hunger Appeal. We couldn't resist the opportunity: the money people paid to shed pounds we would use to feed the hungry of the world. This was registration day for the new term, and all these people who were coming now were signing up for the program. Why so many people? The new course had not been advertised, nor had an elite corps of salesmen invaded the community. There was only one reason why so many people were there that morning. People who had taken the course and had achieved results had shared the good news with their friends. This spontaneous kind of witness had been convincing and effective. Without attempting to sell anyone, the graduates' joy and enthusiasm were very persuasive.

I know because one witnessed to me. It happened while I was in the hospital visiting a parishioner. Shortly after I arrived, a friend of the sick person also came to call. As my member introduced me to this friend she said, "Would you believe I once weighed almost 200 pounds?" I answered, "That's hard to believe." "Well, it's true," she continued. As I turned to the friend, I said, "You must have been on some kind of a program." A half hour later she finished telling me about it. I was ready to sign on the dotted line myself. There is no enthusiasm like that of one who has had a marvelous experience and wants to share it with you. This is what I read in the New Testament. Witnessing to the love of God in Jesus Christ our Lord is a spontaneous and joyful experience. The good news is that God has chosen to live among us in the person of his Son who died and rose again that we might experience his salvation. The sharing of that good news with joy and spontaneity is witnessing. It is telling another what Christ and his church means to us.

Can this be done with the same ease that we witness to our success in a weight-reducing program? Let me tell you about a family that did it. Before leaving our community in a business transfer they were among our finest evangelists. They would deny this because they did not see themselves as professional salespersons for Christ. For this reason they never served on our evangelism committee. They claimed they lacked the knowledge and ability to serve in this area. However, when they moved into a new housing development near our church they made it a point to welcome other new neighbors as they arrived. Not only did they visit the new families, but they always carried with them a hot dish or an invitation to a backyard cookout. Subsequently they formed deep and abiding friendships with all. You could always count on them whenever sorrow or sickness invaded any home. When they saw a neighbor in need, whatever it might be, they ministered. They were also able to articulate in a very natural, warm, and refreshing way, what their Lord and their church meant to them. Because their words were accompanied by deeds of love, their witness was seen as authentic. One by one the families in their block began to visit our church; many ultimately attended the pastor's classes, and made a commitment of faith in Christ. In time there were more families in that one single block belonging to our congregation than any other block in the entire community. Imagine a family that considered itself unworthy of the title "evangelist" doing precisely what caused the early church to grow. They loved one another. They met real human needs. They cared about people and they shared in their own words their experience in the faith. That's witnessing. It's not the oppressive task of mastering a technique, but the joyous opportunity of loving in word and deed.

However, it is good to remember that *our* words and deeds don't do it. We must be faithful, but the Holy Spirit alone can use our witness to light the flame and create faith when and where he wills. Isn't that what Luther wrote many years ago in the Small Catechism? "I believe that I cannot by my own reason or strength believe in Jesus Christ my Lord or come to him. But the Holy Spirit has called me through the gospel, enlightened me with his gifts, and sanctified and preserved me in the true faith." God forbid that we should ever forget that the Holy

Spirit is the energizing power who enables us to witness and enables another to believe. Otherwise we are as weak and powerless as the signalman who unwittingly causes a tragic accident.

Near my boyhood home was the main line of the Northern Pacific Railroad. Where it intersected with a major highway a crossing guard was on duty. Before the days of the automatic signal gates and the ringing bells his task was to warn cars of approaching trains. One night at such a crossing a terrible accident occurred. A young couple and their children were returning home and drove directly into the side of a speeding train. All were instantly killed. At the trial the crossing guard was put on the stand. The prosecuting attorney began his interrogation:

"Were you on duty that evening?"

"Yes, sir."

"Were you awake?"

"Yes, sir."

"Did you see the train coming down the track?"

"Yes, sir."

"Did you take your stop sign and lantern and take your post in front of the track?"

"Yes, sir."

"Did you hold your sign in the air?"

"Yes, sir."

"Did you wave your lantern back and forth?"

"Yes, sir."

With a shrug of the shoulders, the attorney concluded: "No further questions."

It remained a mystery how the driver of the car could miss such obvious signals and hit that train. Many years later the crossing guard, now an old man, guilt-ridden by an agonizing conscience, finally admitted to a close friend, "You know, that prosecuting attorney never asked me if my lantern was lit."

What a tragedy in the church if we ever forget the energizing power of the Holy Spirit. Our Lord promises that when the Holy Spirit has come upon you, "then you shall be my witnesses . . . to the ends of the earth."

It is not my witness, not the cleverness of my words, nor the persuasive power of my argument, or even my deeds of love to a person in need. It is the power of God's Spirit working through the Word which inspires faith. That Word may be the incarnate Lord Jesus Christ himself. That Word may be the Scriptures through which he speaks. That Word may be Christian people who become living epistles as they embody the good news. That Word may be our verbal witness. But whatever form it takes, it is the Word which the Holy Spirit uses in order to strike fire and create faith. What a relief to know that this is his task. It means that we don't have to go out with an oppressive burden, depending on our skills and abilities to persuade others. Rather, motivated by our love of Christ who first loved us, we can make a joyful witness to our faith and Christian experience and leave the rest up to God. The Holy Spirit then uses this in his own way to inspire faith.

With the same freedom and joy of those who shared the good news, "Billy's awake! Praise the Lord!" we are called to bear our witness to the greater reality, "Jesus lives." What a privilege to share what Christ and his church mean in our lives. Not obligation, but opportunity.

How Far Can You Go with Christian Freedom?

JAMES STEPHENSON
Holy Trinity Lutheran Church
Hickory, North Carolina

The police stopped a camper. They demanded the occupants exit and spread-eagle themselves outside the van. The police searched the camper for possible drugs. While the search was underway a car stopped. The driver joined those spread-eagled against the van and asked, "What's making it tip, anyway?"

Ever so many have joined the Christian movement without knowing exactly what is going on. Especially when it comes to the exercise of Christian freedom. The man's real question to the occupants of the van is: "How far can you go with Christian freedom?"

To explore that question we need to take a look at the Magna Charta of Christian freedom, Paul's letter to the Galatians. A short letter, probably the first one Paul wrote. Paul is responding to the attacks made upon what he believes, who he is.

Paul was under attack by a certain kind of Jewish Christian, one who knew the Jews were a chosen people. They believed "You must become Jewish before you become Christian!" How do you do that? Be circumcised. For Paul this implies you could earn the favor of God by doing certain things to your body, and obeying certain rules and regulations.

For Paul the only way to get right with God was faith. For Paul this meant throwing oneself unconditionally on the free mercy of God, as Abraham had done with his son and in going to a distant land. This position troubled this Jewish Christian. It implied more freedom than he felt he could manage. For Paul the question is posed, How far can you go with Christian freedom?

Paul wrote Galatians in response to that question. He says that the law defines sin, thereby making us conscious of sin. But the law cannot cure sin. Only the freedom of faith resolves our broken relationship with God. The Christian therefore has complete freedom from the law. Does that mean you can, as a Christian, do what you like? No, because Christian freedom is conditioned by your sense of responsibility to others, and your love for Jesus. You are free to do anything in Christ! Christian freedom is the freedom to serve humanity and love God.

Recall Paul's listing: illustrations of the fruit of the Spirit, maxims for life in community, a realized but attainable future, Christian life in the new church, specific admonitions for Christian living! These marks of Christian living pose an answer to the question, How far can you go with Christian love? Take care of the one who fails, bear one another's burdens, whatever a man sows, he will reap, let us do good to all men. The fruit of the Spirit is a series of: walking together, restoring the fallen, bearing burdens, sharing all good things.

"If we live by the Spirit, let us also walk by the Spirit," says Paul in Galatians. *Walk*—the word in English takes color from its context: baseball, walking the floor, walking the plank, walking in step. "Keep in step with one's fellows" was the Greek meaning of the word for Paul. Walking in the Spirit, the Christian is a well-disciplined person, trained to keep in step with his fellows. The same Greek word is also used of dancers as they go through the complex choreography of religious drama. You can walk together in your Christian freedom, with the Spirit of God. You are free to walk together in Christ as far as you want to go.

For far too long we have ignored this basic fact of life, saying that the Christian life can be lived only in solitude. Even the ancient Simeon Stylites, who spent so many years sitting on top of a pillar, could not have lasted long without the admiring crowds below witnessing his performance. Christian freedom shouts, "We are in this together!"

In it as Christians together, with the father with his hand on the door of the city morgue, looking for a son who didn't come home last night. In it as Christians together, with the neighbor sitting on his bed, toying with a pistol. In it as Christians together, with a young woman being wheeled into the hospital delivery room knowing it would be her life or her child's. In it as Christians together, eating breakfast and catching a glimpse of the world's hungry. My Christian freedom means we are in it together! You can go as far as you can with this freedom.

An important part of life together is the rescue squad. The doctor may deplore the accident that caused the broken leg, but he knows why he is there. He is there to set the broken leg. The word Paul uses for *restore* is the same technical term used for setting a broken bone. In our life together relationships are strained, fractures occur. Paul says to take care of the one who fails. You can go as far as you can with this Christian freedom.

Howard K. Smith is one of my favorite news commentators. Characteristically, he commented on the New York blackout by noting the fear and crime, and the help New York is not getting. His story concluded with a picture of the hospital emergency rooms as battlegrounds. Not a new observation for him.

Howard K. Smith, with many others, fled Berlin in the hours before World War II broke out. At one point the Gestapo boarded the train, singled out Howard K. Smith, and ordered him to empty his pockets. The Gestapo officer ordered other officers to join him as he pondered a document from Howard K. Smith's pocket. The document from his pocket was a sermon on the text, "Bear one another's burdens, and so fulfill the law of Christ." It was a wedding sermon by a Lutheran pastor in Munich, delivered as he officiated at the marriage of his young vicar. Shortly after the wedding the pastor was picked up by the Gestapo for resistance.

Howard K. Smith spent two days and nights in a Nazi jail for having that pastor's sermon in his pocket. While in jail himself, Howard K. Smith reflected on the wedding occasion. He remembered asking the bride for a copy of the sermon in which the pastor, now in prison, had said to the young couple, from Galatians 6:2, "You will probably be the only one of the three pastors of this eight-thousand-member church in freedom. Nearly every family has heartaches and burdens. There are wives and children who have no income because the Nazi jails have their husbands and fathers. You are fulfilling the law of Christ in sharing their burdens." Then the pastor turned to the young bride and said, "You will see your husband come home at night tired beyond belief. It is then you are to minister to the minister."

Bear one another's burdens! The Gestapo let Howard K. Smith go. The pastor who preached that sermon died in a concentration camp! Both Howard K. Smith and that pastor are free in Christ!

The New Evangelism

RALPH J. WALLACE
St. Paul's Lutheran Church
Columbia, South Carolina

For the followers of Jesus his resurrection was not a climax that cleanly completed everything. His resurrection was not a stupendous summation that enabled them to sigh with relief because all the loose ends had been tied in a neat bundle. Rather, for the followers of Jesus, his resurrection was a further fact in a continuously climbing climax. His resurrection was a proving peak, a heartening high point, an invigorating impetus that sent them on to the continuous climax of Christianizing the world. The resurrection of Jesus was the ending of darkness and the beginning of light, the ending of death and the beginning of life that his followers were to make available to all men.

The church always has known that the resurrection of Jesus is not a crashing climax that stops and seals the activity like a sounding cymbal at the end of a symphony. The church always has known that the resurrection of Jesus is a glorious gift to be given to the world. So the church has been involved in evangelism.

Unfortunately there has been an erosion of evangelism, a corruption in carrying Christ's gift to others, a perversion in the practice of Christianizing the world. During the greater part of the church's history of work in foreign missions, evangelism has meant the Westernization of foreign lands before the Christianization of them. Their lifestyles had to be changed to match ours before they could be renewed spiritually. Naked persons had to put on clothes and polygamous persons had to put away all their wives but one before they could be Christian. Thank goodness, now we are more concerned about Christianization than Westernization.

We have not been so fortunate at home. Our approach to others has been, and to a large extent still is, selfish. We have said to others, "Add your strength to ours and we shall become the largest and most influential church in town. We shall be able to raise a beautiful building. We shall be able to employ a large staff and provide good programs for our children. We need you because you can do so much for us." It is that continuing method of outreach, witness, evangelism, or whatever you want to call it that forces us to look at our background Scripture and see the new evangelism.

The first step in the new evangelism is seen in John's statement that "Jesus came and stood among them." God's evangelism always has begun with his coming and standing among people. He stood with Israel in the cloud and pillar of fire. He stood with Israel's kings in the prophets. He stood with the people of the world in Israel and in a Man born in the line of David. So it isn't surprising to see Jesus coming and standing among his fearful followers.

God always had made it a point to come to people in need. When Jacob was at odds with his brother Esau, God came to him in a comforting dream. When Isaiah was wrestling with his call, God came to him in a temple experience. When Simeon was old and in danger of dying without seeing the Messiah, God came to him in Mary's son who was to be blessed. So it is not surprising to find Jesus coming into the upper room that was filled with leaderless followers, anxious followers, bewildered followers, followers who had left everything and who wondered if their lives too would be taken, or if Jesus would come back to them as he promised. Jesus came to those persons in need and stood among them, and his coming was the first step in God's evangelism.

Our coming and standing among persons is the first step in the new evangelism. Evangelism doesn't happen when a staff of professional visitors are paid to call on prospective members. Evangelism doesn't happen when a committee is appointed to recruit reluctant visitors, to produce an elaborate plan for canvassing a community, and to require a filled-out card to be filed showing that a call has been made. Evangelism happens when a person of love goes to a person in need and openly, warmly, and generously implies that he is present to help, and asks what need he can meet. You and I, the evangelists, must come among them. We must stand among them. That is the only way their need can be discerned, the only way their need can be met, and the only way that they can see Christ: in our being there to help. Coming and standing among them is the first step in the new evangelism.

The second step in the new evangelism can be seen in John's statement that "Jesus came and stood among them and said to them, 'Peace be with you.'" God's evangelistic efforts always have involved a coming with peace. His coming and standing among people has been for the purpose of producing peace, not war. When God called Abraham out of Ur, he was not calling him into the warlike life of a nomad, to fight with elements and people for survival. He was saying, "Peace be with you. I will make your descendants as numerous as the stars in the sky, as the sand grains on the shore, and they will be my people to light the world." When God put accuracy in David's sling-arm and strength in Samson's hair, he wasn't just getting rid of the enemy by causing them to kill people. He was saying to them, "Peace be with you. If you will be my people, I will be your God." When Jesus spoke sharply to the Syrophoenician woman, drove the corrupters from the temple, and rebuked the sleepyheaded disciples in Gethsemane, he was saying, "Peace be with you." Peace comes from a built-up faith, from being in the temple as a house of prayer, from praying that you enter not into temptation. God's evangelism is peculiar in its second step. It appears to be war, but it is really his way of saying, "Peace be with you." The upper room crowd may have expected to have been reamed-out by the risen Lord for their cowardice. But there he was, proclaiming peace.

The second step in the new evangelism requires us to be more obvious than God. When we come and stand among others we must clearly say, "Peace be with you." Our approach to problem-packing and need-needled persons is not to be one of attack. We are not to say to the alcoholic, "Quit drinking, and all will be well;" or to the poor, "Get a job, and things will be better;" or to the faithless, "Only believe, and all things will be added unto you;" or to the confused, "If you will read your Bible, you will find that you have pat answers to all your questions;" or to the hypochondriac, "You just think you are sick." That kind of war-making only gets us further from the problem-packing and need-needled person, and further from the truth. Our approach is to be one of "Peace be with you." Why do you feel the need for alcohol? Why are you in these financial straits? What is the condition of your faith? What kind of answers do you find in the Scriptures? Why do you feel that you must seek support through sickness? That is "Peace be with you," the question-asking that means interest and a desire to help. That is the second step in the new evangelism.

The third step in the new evangelism can be seen in John's statement that "Jesus came and stood among them and said to them 'Peace be with you' and . . . showed them his hands and side." God's evangelism always has involved his presenting his credentials, his giving evidence of the reason for proclaiming peace instead of making war. In the ark of the covenant in the holy of holies in the wilderness tabernacle, the Israelites kept the budding rod of Aaron that had been given through Moses at the time of the Exodus to prove that God was doing something for Israel. The budding rod that could be cast down and changed into a snake to consume the snake of the Egyptian magicians was God's credential. It showed him to be a God of love who did love. The bronze serpent in the wilderness was a similar symbol. It reminded Israel of the sin that brought the snakes, but it also reminded Israel of the forgiving Father. When they looked at it they remembered and were healed. The continuing Passover was God's credential. Annually the children were reminded that their God delivered them. So it wasn't so strange that Jesus presented his hands and side. They were his credentials, the evidence of what kind of person he was. Those holes held up the fact that Jesus was love, the same love that had spoken softly and sharply, that had touched tenderly and healingly, that had died willingly. The third step in God's evangelism always has involved the evidence of love.

That means our new evangelism must involve some credential showing, some evidence of sharing, some marks of love. In our going and standing with and saying, "Peace be with you," there should be some willingness to listen that we have learned from our own need to be heard; some willingness to share that springs from our own need to be shared with; some willingness to serve that shoots up from the realization that we have been served; some willingness to love that leaps from our knowledge that we are loved. These marks from life, these wounds of love that have come from our Lord and through us to others, should be held out as evidence of our seriousness and sincerity in standing among others and saying to them, "Peace be with you." That credential giving is a necessary third step in the new evangelism.

The fourth and final step in the new evangelism can be seen in John's statement that "Jesus came and stood among them and said to them, 'Peace be with you' . . . and showed them his hands and side. Jesus said to them again, 'Peace be with you.'" "Jesus said to them again, 'Peace be with you.'" There never has been in God's evangelism any open hostility or smoldering resentment at having to present the credentials of love. There never has been any animosity toward those who require the mark of love. God must have been pained at the need of a flood, but in the rainbow he was saying to man again, "Peace be with you." His countenance must have been scarred by a second forty years in the wilderness, but he said even to disobedient Moses, "Peace be with you," you can look into the promised land. If God has any anthropomorphic feelings, they must have been hurt when Israel rejected the prophets sent by him. But there he was saying, "Peace be with you." Saul shall be your king. Ebedmelech, go and take Jeremiah out of the cistern so that he can prophesy again. There was no wrath in the voice of Jesus as he met with his almost-crumbled church. There was no ill will expressed, no "look what you have done to me" attitude. He showed his credentials and said again, "Peace be with you."

That step in God's evangelism, that repeated recalling to reconciliation in a tone of love, is the final step in our new evangelism.

Martyrdom is great, but a martyr's complex is grotesque. Displaying the credentials of love is constructive, but complaining about them is destructive. Wearing the marks of love to free others is commendable, but using them to enslave or indebt others is damnable. One marriage mate doesn't help the other by bemoaning the demands of their marriage. He or she helps the other by joyfully bearing them, by saying, "Peace be with you." That is the crowning climax to our evangelistic efforts—letting others know that we joyfully bear the burdens of love, as frequently as necessary, that we resiliently return, saying to those being evangelized, "Peace be with you."

The church of Jesus Christ needs to turn to a new evangelism, or better yet, to the old evangelism practiced by our Lord.

We need to come and stand among persons of need, not attacking but assuring that we come in peace. We need to offer the evidence of our love, not to bind others through a sense of indebtedness but to build up with our peaceful assurance of continued acceptance.

Lutheran Evangelism: Is There a Difference?

WILLIAM S. WAXENBERG
St. Luke Lutheran Church
Spokane, Washington

I'm a Lutheran pastor. I know that is not unique among those of us gathered here, but I would venture to say that I am the only Lutheran pastor here who started out as a Jew and thought about becoming a Roman Catholic priest before being ordained into the gospel ministry!

Let me elaborate. My father was Jewish. My mother was a Methodist when she married my father. Her mother had been a Baptist and her father a Cumberland Presbyterian. She converted to Judaism and if anyone would have ever told them their only child would grow up to be a Lutheran pastor, they certainly wouldn't have believed it!

As I was growing up we celebrated both the Jewish and Christian holidays, I suspect out of deference to my mother's Christian background. We always had a Christmas tree which, I understand, was to be given up when I started Sunday school. I don't think my father realized that one does not take a Christmas tree away from a five-year-old.

We belonged to, and attended regularly, the local Reform synagogue. My parents went to services every Friday evening, and I went once a month on children's night. I attended Sunday school for two hours every Sunday morning.

When I was in fourth grade I began attending Hebrew school once a week to prepare for my bar mitzvah, which is a Jewish ceremony meaning "son of the covenant." It is at this point in a Jewish boy's life that he becomes an adult member of the congregation. My bar mitzvah training was interrupted, however, in the fifth grade when I broke my leg playing football. I landed in the hospital for six and one-half weeks and was laid up at home for another six. Also during this time my father died from heart disease. Since I had missed a good share of my second year in Hebrew school, my mother did not insist that I go back, and thus I was never bar mitzvahed. I did continue in Sunday school and at age sixteen went through a one-year confirmation program and was confirmed. Like many of our young people in the church, after confirmation I never went back.

As I grew I always believed in God, had an idea of Jesus (all my friends were Christians), and could have best been described as a Pharisaic moralist. I cannot tell you at what point Jesus Christ intersected my life as a Person. As I look back I realize it happened gradually. I do know that during the summer between my junior and senior years in high school I became very interested in Roman Catholicism. We had close family friends who were Irish Roman Catholics, and I suppose the influence came from them. At the same time I saw a movie on television entitled *A Man Called Peter*, the story of the Presbyterian minister Peter Marshall. I thus developed an interest in the ministry—although I didn't know what it entailed beyond public speaking, which I enjoyed—but that, combined with my interest in Roman Catholicism, led me to decide I would become a priest!

During my senior year of high school I met a young lady who was to later become my wife. Carol and her family were Christian Scientists, and as a promising, young Jewish Roman Catholic influenced for the priesthood by a Presbyterian minister, we did not see eye-to-eye on religion. One thing we did agree on, however, and that was the importance of a relationship with God. We knew that if our relationship with each other was to last we needed to get together on the same theological plane. And besides, even though I wanted to be a priest, I could not convince Carol to become a nun!

When I went off to college I began church shopping. I worshiped at the Methodist, Presbyterian, and Roman Catholic churches with little satisfaction. One weekend when I was home we worshiped at a large Lutheran church near to where we lived. That service struck a responsive chord. I didn't know much about the Lutheran church, but the liturgy and the sermon seemed to say this is where we belonged.

Toward the end of my first year in college I was yet without a major because I didn't know what I wanted to do with my life. I hadn't thought much about the ministry for some time, but one evening as I was alone studying I began to think about where I was headed. There were no flashing lights or voices but right then and there I was convinced the ministry was my calling. I have never been as certain of anything else in my life. I was so excited that I hurried back to the fraternity house to write a letter home, and as I approached the door one of my fraternity brothers said, "Well if it isn't Rev. Waxenberg!" I was dumbfounded! How did he know?

The next time I was home I made an appointment to see the pastor of the Lutheran church where we had worshiped. The pastor's name was Emerson Miller, and he was a wonderful, loving, understanding man. When I sat down in his office I blurted out something like, "I've got a problem. I'm a Jew whose father was Jewish, whose mother is of Baptist, Presbyterian, and Methodist background, and I've been interested in Roman Catholicism and have been influenced by a now dead Presbyterian minister to become a Catholic priest, and I'm going with a Christian Scientist and I've just been called into the Lutheran ministry! What do I do?" Emerson Miller was unflappable. I don't remember much of what he said, but he never questioned my sincerity. He accepted me as I was and merely suggested that when I was home for the summer I come to a pastor's class, which I did with my wife-to-be and my mother. On October 16, 1966 I was baptized into the Christian faith.

I tell you all of this not to lift up myself, but in order that you might know something of who I am, because that colors what I want to say this morning. I also tell you my story because my story, like your story, is a part of God's story, the climax of which are his mighty acts in Jesus Christ. The Christ-event is, then, the focal point of our attention, for he is the foundation upon which we build our theology, our programs, our lifestyles. It is precisely because of what God has done in Jesus Christ and is yet doing through the power and presence of his Holy Spirit that we are even here this morning. Let us keep that foremost in our minds as we approach our topic, "Lutheran Evangelism: Is There a Difference?" I would like to answer that in typical Lutheran fashion: yes and no.

On the one hand, it matters not whether Lutheran evangelism differs from other kinds because God has not called us to be different; we have been called to be faithful, faithful in the task of witnessing by word and deed to the mighty acts of God in Jesus Christ. We can be assured that God does not sit upon his throne pondering the differences in evangelistic approaches between the Baptists and the Presbyterians, the Roman Catholics and Lutherans. And therefore, why should we? Whether we as Lutherans are different from our brothers and sisters in Christ whose denominational titles are unlike ours is neither important nor significant. And to try and ferret out the differences because we don't "want to be like them" is not a profitable thing to do.

On the other hand, the topic "Lutheran Evangelism: Is There a Difference?" is excellent because it forces us as Lutheran Christians to examine, or perhaps reexamine our theology of evangelism, regardless of whether or not we are different. We certainly need to know ourselves and understand the task to which we have been called. We need to know just what it is that we as Lutheran Christians believe about evangelism. What do we believe are the roots of our evangelical task? In what kind of soil are these roots planted? How can we best nurture these roots in order that they might grow into plants and bear fruit? What kind of fruit ought we to be cultivating? These and other questions spring forth from "Lutheran Evangelism: Is There a Difference?" Therefore, I would like to suggest that the soil from which Lutheran evangelism springs is composed of six characteristics.

Lutheran evangelism is first of all biblical. That means two things: we have a history; and we have a story to tell. Our history and thus our story go all the way back to the beginning, back to when "the earth was without form and void and darkness was on the face of the deep" (Gen. 1:2), back to when God said, "'Let there be light,' and there was light" (Gen. 1:3). Our faith story as Lutheran Christians does not begin in 1619 when the first Lutherans came to North America; nor does it begin in 1517 at the church in Wittenberg; nor does it even begin in 33 A.D. on a windswept hill outside Jerusalem. Our story goes back to the time when there was nothing, and God created something out of it.

Our story as Christians is to be found in the entire Scripture, not just the New Testament. We need only read the Gospel According to Matthew, or Paul's Letter to the church at Rome, or the Letter to the Hebrews to realize how conscious the early church was of its faith roots. The church's story is rooted in the story of Israel, our forefathers in the faith.

And our story is the story of God, because he is at the center. He is the one that is revealed in the story of Israel and the story of the church. It is he to whom all Scripture points, a God who is ultimate in authority and yet who dialogues with his creation, a God who forgives the sins of his people and yet himself repents, a God who is jealous and yet has infinite patience, a God who hates evil so much that he is filled with a passionate self-giving love which propels him to take up residence among his creation in the person Jesus of Nazareth.

It is vitally important that we grasp the history and story of God and his people as recounted in the Scriptures because so many today are filled with false visions of who this God is and what he does. There is a story told about a young man stationed in a war zone. Because of what he was called upon to do he was burdened with intense guilt feelings that would manifest themselves whenever he walked past the base chapel. Instead of walking directly past the building that symbolized the God of love in the midst of his suffering world, he would walk way out and around the chapel to avoid what he believed was an angry God who was ready to strike him down should he venture too close.

That image of God is false because it is inconsistent with the God whose story is told in the Scriptures. That's why it is so important for us to know our faith story, God's story. That is why it is so vital for us to be biblical in our evangelism.

We Lutherans are not only biblical; we are, in the second place, also creedal. This is vitally important for us because the Apostles', Nicene, and Athanasian creeds remind us that we are created, redeemed, and sustained by one God. The creeds reaffirm for us what was so important to our fathers of the faith in Israel: a strict monotheism, a firm belief that there was only one true, living God. Such a creed expresses itself in the prayer: "Hear O Israel, the Lord our God, the Lord is one" (Deut. 6:4).

The creeds of the church remind us of this great truth. Even though our understanding of the nature of God differs from that of ancient Israel, in that we believe God has revealed himself in three distinct Persons, yet we acknowledge that is only one God.

The creeds, then, preserve us from two dangers. One is to believe and worship God apart from his revelation as Father, Son, and Holy Spirit. God is a personal God above all else. Several years ago I worked in a men's clothing store with a girl who one day remarked to me that she believed in God, but "that was about it." The creeds prevent us from saying such things. They guard against that popular belief that God is a Supreme Being "out there" somewhere. Such a belief is certainly comfortable and safe because it means God does not have to be reckoned with. I can live my life anyway I please. I can do my own thing without any accountability to the creating, redeeming, sanctifying God. The creeds keep us from such self-indulgence because they remind us that the one and only God has chosen to become intimate with his creation. He then chooses to get involved. He has chosen of his own free will not only to create, but to penetrate his creation, live among it, and experience all that his creation experiences —even death.

The second great danger from which the monotheistic creeds keep us is the everpresent inclination to worship the Father *or* the Son *or* the Holy Spirit apart from the other two. It has been said that the emphasis in the Lutheran church has been on the Father, the emphasis of the Baptists on the Son, and the emphasis of the Pentecostals on the Holy Spirit. Emphasis leads to worship.

When I was in seminary we had a guest speaker come and talk. She said she was a witch. I can remember only two things that she said: (1) most witches are good, and (2) witches have their own form of worship which includes, she said, a holy trilogy. When she said *trilogy* instead of *trinity* I thought she was just ignorant. Now I wonder if perhaps she was prophetic, for a trilogy is a set of three separate stories linked by a common theme, allowing for a preference and a selection of one over the other two. There is a tendency in the church to believe in a trilogy, not a trinity, to believe in three separate and distinct gods, preferring one over the other, instead of believing in one God who reveals himself in three Persons.

As Lutheran Christians, we stand firm on the creeds of the church. We are trinitarian in our expression and we are monotheists in our belief. The creeds remind us of that.

Lutherans are not only biblical and creedal; we are also, in the third place, confessional. That of course means many things, but without going into the entire Book of Concord which contains the confessions of the Lutheran church, it seems that the heart of the confessions is Luther's theology of the cross, as over against a theology of glory. If those are new terms for you, let me explain it this way: the theology of glory wishes to know God only in all of his majesty, in all of his grandeur, in the beauty of nature, and in the face of the angels. The theology of the cross, however, sees God in the suffering of the world, especially in the pain and humiliation of Calvary.

It is against these two theologies that Lutheran evangelism must be measured. Our confessions do not allow us to invite people into the Christian community in the belief that now all of life will be grand; that now that one is a Christian, now that one is saved, life is sunshine, lollipops, and roses; for it is as Bonhoeffer wrote: "When Christ calls a man, he bids him to come and die."

You will remember that when a person is baptized in the Lutheran church the pastor makes the sign of the cross on the forehead of the one being baptized, and these words are spoken: "Receive the sign of the holy cross, that henceforth you will know the Lord, the power of his resurrection, *and* the fellowship of his suffering." Our confessions enable us to understand that the call of Christ is to pick up the cross and follow after him—to give of ourselves for his sake and for the sake of others.

Lest I be misunderstood, let me hasten to add that this does not mean we preach doom and gloom. Quite the contrary. We preach the joy and hope of the resurrection, and it is in that light that we see the cross. But we do see it. It is yet there and it will not go away. Therefore when I am called into the fellowship of the church I enter a life of service to those both inside *and* outside the church. I repent, that is, I turn away from myself and back toward the God who reveals himself in the cross of his Son.

Such an understanding of Lutheran evangelism leads us to the fourth characteristic: Lutheran evangelism is wholistic. It ministers to the whole person. This means that we meet the needs of people where they are. "A hungry stomach cannot hear," and thus we do not proclaim salvation of the soul to one who is dying of hunger. That is why Lutheran evangelism must walk hand in hand with social ministry, stewardship, and all the thrusts of the church. Those of us involved in evangelism cannot sit back and say we have no obligation to feed the hungry of the world because we are involved in saving their souls. When we do that we again hear the voice of our Lord echoing from the temple: "The Spirit of the Lord is upon me because he has anointed me to preach good news to the poor. He has sent me to proclaim release to the captives and recovering of sight to the blind, to set at liberty those who are oppressed, to proclaim the acceptable year of the Lord" (Luke 4:18-19).

We stand in error if we overspiritualize this to the point where we become blind to the physical needs of others, for with the coming of Jesus Christ we are compelled to see the world and all therein in a new light because the New Age has already begun.

In the sixties the church's social consciousness overshadowed the spiritual concern of humankind. We must not allow the reverse to happen in the seventies and eighties and nineties. Our faith is not a matter of choosing one over the other, evangelism over social concern, or vice versa. The two walk hand in hand because evangelism itself is declaring by word *and* deed the mighty acts of God in Jesus Christ.

Besides being wholistic, Lutheran evangelism is also individualistic. God views each of us as an individual, unique in personality, strengths, and weaknesses, and this brings each of us to the cross in his own way.

Earlier I mentioned my religious experience, my faith story as to how I came into the church. For me to say or even imply that my experience should be yours would be heresy pure and simple. My experience cannot be yours and yours cannot be mine because I am not you and you are not me. When we reach out with the good news we must always remember there is no one else like us.

We are living in an age where everything must be experienced to be appreciated. Everyone is looking for new experiences, and the prevailing belief is that if you have not had an identifiable religious experience, you're not in. There is a man in our congregation who had a particular religious experience three years ago. It changed his life. He needed that experience to turn him around. Another man in our congregation came to me saying he hoped he would have a similar experience. He felt inadequate in his faith and believed a "shaking of the foundations" would make him more faithful. But that man will probably never have such an experience, at least one like the first man had, because God is dealing with two very different people.

I suspect the failure to see people as individuals is what prompted Paul to delineate the different gifts of the Spirit in 1 Corinthians 12. For by the grace of God I am what I am and you are who you are, and God takes that into account when he confronts us in our lives.

Some Christians will never have any identifiable religious experiences. Others will have many. We must never cast one out as unfaithful in favor of the other. God meets people where they are, not where we think they should be.

Sixth and last, we Lutheran Christians are corporate. That is, we have been created—and saved—for the sake of others, and thus as we evangelize we invite people to become a part of congregational life, because the church is the visible manifestation of the invisible, risen body of Christ.

We need to understand this, and so do the people to whom we bring the good news. We've all heard people say, "I can be just as good a Christian without belonging to the church." At that point I want to narrow the use of the word Christian. A person can be a good person without the church, but a person cannot be a Christian without the church. Now that's not a very popular stance, but I am willing to take it because I believe the church is our link to the risen Lord. It is here, in the context of community worship, that we remember his mighty acts, that we hear his Word, that we celebrate his presence among us.

We can acknowledge that the church is imperfect; that yes, this is where the hypocrites are; that yes, we have sinners here too. And no, we are not any better than the people who aren't in the church. But we are forgiven and reconciled to God through Christ our Lord, and we have accepted that forgiveness, and we participate in the life and mission of the Christian community.

The task of Lutheran evangelism is to declare by word and deed the mighty acts of God in Jesus Christ, and to invite people to share in the life and mission of the church, his body. The church is God's gift to a broken world, a gift wherein we find reconciling love, wholeness through forgiveness, strength and guidance for life. To be a Christian and to be the church go hand in hand.

"Lutheran Evangelism: Is There a Difference?" Yes and no, for we are biblical, creedal, and confessional. We are wholistic, individualistic, and corporate. And the foundation that undergirds them all is the Lord God who "in many and various ways spoke of old to our fathers through the prophets, but in these last days He has spoken to us by a Son" (Heb. 1:1–2). So be it.

Every Man Has a Burning Bush

PAUL M. WERGER
St. Luke's Lutheran Church
Bloomington, Minnesota

I suppose that every one of us has a secret desire to have an experience like Moses' on Mt. Horeb. We ask ourselves the question, "Why doesn't God show me a burning bush?"

And you must admit that it would be far easier to know the will of God for our lives if only we could see a light and hear a voice like Saul did on the road to Damascus, or have a temple vision like Isaiah, or catch a miraculous catch of fish like Peter did on the Sea of Galilee.

Keith Miller tells the story of an outstanding layman who was very dissatisfied with his Christian experience. Since he was successful and well-to-do he decided to tour the holy sites to see if he could gather inspiration from them.

He went to England and to Aldersgate Street where John Wesley's heart was "strangely warmed." Next he went to Wittenberg, Germany to visit the Augustinian seminary where Luther had seen the light and "the gates of heaven clicked open at his feet." Then he went to Rome to stand at St. Peter's Church where it was reputed Peter had been crucified upside down. He went to the Holy Land and stood on the Mount of Transfiguration, at Calvary where Jesus was crucified, and at the Garden Tomb where the resurrection took place. He even went to Mt. Horeb where Moses saw the burning bush.

But he came home very disappointed. Those places were just normal, natural, everyday places. God had used the commonplace and the ordinary to accomplish his purposes.

What was so extraordinary was that men had come face to face with themselves and with their God. They had given themselves completely to God, and that had made all the difference. So he concluded that there had been many burning bushes in his life as well.

He could recall his confirmation day when God seemed closer to him than at any time in his life. He thought of the first awakening to the tender, sweet love of his wife, and the precious gift God had given him. He recalled the moment he looked through the nursery window at his first son, and knew God had wrought another miracle. He thought of last fall when he stood at his father's graveside and felt peace like he had never known before.

Yes, he had had many experiences in God as well. So it was little wonder that when they asked him to preach on Layman's Sunday about his experience in the holy sites of the world that he entitled his sermon "Any Old Bush Will Do," and tried to relate how every man has been like Moses at the burning bush.

Now I would like each of you to sit back this morning and think about the many burning bushes in your life. I know that some of you may protest that you have never seen a burning bush, nor have you ever heard God's voice call out your name from it. But I would ask all of you to think this through again.

I know a man who has a hard time believing in God at all. In his difficulty he became a victim of drink and had to be hospitalized. Even though he wasn't an active member of his church, his pastor called on him each week. He remarked to his wife that he just couldn't understand why that pastor had bothered with him and shown him this kind of love.

He failed to realize that God was giving him a burning bush experience, calling his name through that pastor. Any God who comes to us through bread and wine, comes also through his servants.

Or I think about the parents who have been the burning bush for their children by seeing that they were brought to God in baptism, confirmation, Sunday school, and church.

I am very amazed at the number of adults who never realize that God was speaking to them through their parents. "My parents made me go to church when I was a child and I won't go to church now— I've had enough to last me a lifetime."

But how many of us would be here today if it were not for our parents acting like the burning bush for each of us? All we have to do is think of St. Monica's prayers for her son Augustine, or Hannah's prayers for Samuel. John Wesley said about his mother Suzannah: "I learned more about Christianity from my mother than from all the theologians of England."

I wonder if many of us aren't seeing the burning bush or hearing God call our name when we are asked to speak to another about him. For Jesus commissioned every baptized person to go on his behalf and speak to every person who does not acknowledge him. He calls us where we are and uses ordinary people just like ourselves to be his witnesses.

There is the sense that we are on holy ground when the pastor or some lay leader invites us to participate. It may not be thunder or lightning from heaven, but that "still small voice" of God that speaks to our spirit and says, "John, Mary, Sue, or Bill, go for me. Tell them about my love and salvation." It may be happening to us now for are we not on "holy ground" as we worship and isn't it true that "where two or three are gathered together in my name, I am in the midst of them"?

I think that people realize this subconsciously. That is one of the reasons we usually sit in the back at a church service or shrink into the shadows to escape responsibility. At times such as these we cannot escape. Every man has a burning bush.

"Wait a moment," some will say, "it is just not the same. That bush was not consumed. I have never seen anything like that and I doubt if I ever will." I find that this is the basic fear that church members have of God and their church. They are afraid that they will be consumed if they say yes to God.

I doubt if Moses would have been so anxious to examine that burning bush if he knew what God had in store for him. "Moses," says God, "I see the plight of my children in Egypt. I'll send you to Pharaoh to lead the children out of bondage."

But Moses didn't want to go to Pharaoh. He had killed an Egyptian and Pharaoh was after him. "Who am I to go to Pharaoh?" protested Moses.

"It's OK," says God, "I will go with you and watch over you."

"But the Israelites won't believe me—who shall I say sent me?"

God replies, "Just tell them that I am the God of Abraham, Isaac, and Jacob. Say that my name is *I Am*. I Am has sent me."

"But," says Moses, "they will say 'I can't believe you.'"

God says, "Stretch out your rod," and suddenly it becomes a snake. "Now grab it by the tail," and it becomes his rod again.

"But, Lord, I am not eloquent. I can't speak," says Moses.

"I will give you your brother Aaron for a spokesman," declares God.

Doesn't it all sound too familiar. Moses was afraid he would be consumed in serving God. He forgot that it was the great I Am who sent him. And isn't that just like us!

"Will you be a visitor?" we ask. "Please don't ask me, Lord, I can't call. I can't speak. I will be consumed." However, in the background a voice says, "You will not be consumed. I Am has sent you."

If a lake receives water and doesn't give it off, the lake will die and nothing can live in it. If we receive the love and sacrifice of Christ into our lives and don't sacrifice ourselves, we die within.

It is probably easier to give our money than it is to visit someone or witness to our faith. "Lord," we say, "I can't speak. I am not eloquent. They won't believe me."

"Just go," says God. "I Am has sent you."

Samuel Shoemaker, a great Episcopal preacher who is dead now, tells about an early experience he had when he was a young priest teaching in China. He was attracted to a brilliant young Chinese scholar who was a colleague. He knew he should speak to him about Christ, but he felt he could not. So he went to an evangelist he knew and asked him to do the task. "Why don't you speak to him?" the evangelist asked.

"Episcopalians just don't do that," protested Shoemaker.

"I don't believe you," said the evangelist. "I believe the problem is with you and your secret sin." Shoemaker said it was like a knife piercing his heart. "Go home," said the evangelist, "and examine yourself by the standards of purity, honesty, truth, and faithfulness."

Shoemaker did so. For him it was a burning bush experience—he gave himself to Christ in a new way. The next day he went to speak to his Chinese friend. He prayed the whole way there that the friend wouldn't be home. But he was home and Shoemaker spoke to him about Christ and, to his surprise, that man became a Christian. Shoemaker was not consumed. It was the beginning of something great in his life, and it could be your experience too.

I wonder if you haven't been to the burning bush. As you sit here this morning in the quietude of worship, I wonder if God hasn't been calling your name. I am certain this isn't the first time he has called you, but this time it could be different. Remember what that traveler discovered: God had used ordinary men at ordinary places to accomplish his will. What was different was that they had come face to face with God and had given themselves to him.

A London *Times* reporter asked General William Booth, founder of the Salvation Army, what was the secret of his great success. "I guess," said Booth, "God has had all of me that I was capable of giving."

God stands in our temple today saying to each of us as he said to Isaiah: "Who will go for us? Whom shall I send?" May we have the faith and courage to respond: "Here am I. Send me!" And why should we fear? "I Am has sent us."

Evangelism and the Theology of the Cross

RONALD J. LAVIN
St. Paul Lutheran Church
Davenport, Iowa

Some months ago when I was on a road in Colorado, we ran into a traffic jam, and out from the car in front of me came a burly man who responded to the situation like this: "For Christ's sake, what's going on here?" I was offended because of the use of the Lord's name, but then as I thought about the question, I thought about the wide-ranging implications of that question: "For Christ's sake, what is going on here?"

I understand that Trinity Church, Camp Hill, Pennsylvania, left the Central Pennsylvania Synod last year. At least the equivalent of Trinity Church left, as the synod president noted in his report, for over two thousand adults somehow disappeared from the synod's membership rolls. Other synods show similar losses. Of course what is going on for Christ's sake is not explained simply in terms of numbers. Evangelical Outreach is not a numbers game. But declining numbers may be evidence of a need for an emphasis on outreach. I am bold to share with you as a congregation of fellow Christians around the question, "For Christ's sake, what is going on here?" because our churches have not been as effective as they could be.

As we seek to be more efficient evangelists three references from Holy Scripture should prove helpful: "Go out to the whole world and proclaim the good news to all creation" (Mark 16:15); the Exodus passage from the Old Testament about Moses and the coming out of the people of God; and the third chapter of the Gospel of John, where we have reference to that coming out into the wilderness, a snake being held up and people being healed as they beheld what Moses held on a pole.

Evangelism will be done out of one of three different theologies. The first is a theology of bondage. This theology really means that evangelism is not done, for it we believe we are still back in bondage in Egypt, in slavery, it is not likely that we will invite anyone to join us. If we believe that life is nothing more than duty, hard work, and slavery, there is a missing joy that results in a missing witness. We are God's people. By baptism we have been freed from that slavery; we are not in Egypt. But if we believe we are in Egypt it is not likely that we will witness or invite anyone to join us.

William Lazareth made reference to this when he said that Lutherans here in America have generally done evangelism by the means of boats and babies. As people with Lutheran heritage have come over from Europe we have integrated them into our American situation and our American churches. We Lutherans have also tended to have babies. But, Lazareth pointed out, the boats have stopped and the pills have started. We'd better find another way to reach out beyond our membership or we will soon become a Teutonic (or Scandinavian) cult living unto ourselves. Of course he is right. If we believe that we can only reach people like ourselves, we are in bondage and we are in serious trouble.

Part of the problem is that, being sinners, all of us in one form or another are in bondage. I think of my own situation for a moment. Back in 1970 my wife had pneumonia. The doctor said, "Get her to a warm climate." A friend, flying me in a private plane, noted that he and his wife would be going to Florida and they would be glad to have her go along. We made arrangements for my wife and me, and for my friend, his wife, and their two children to fly to Sebring, Florida, and then he would go on to Tampa. They dropped us in Sebring on the last day of 1969. On the first day of 1970, after a friend and I came back from an early morning bike ride, we were greeted by the news that our pilot friend, his wife, and their two children had crashed in Tampa and all were dead. What I did was to immediately go to the assistance of those who were grieving, including my wife and our Florida friends. If someone had told me that I generally was in a role as a pastor and that role was a kind of bondage, I would have denied it. I saw myself as a real person, but in truth I had been so geared up for the pastoral role and doing the pastoral thing, involved in pastoral work, that when it came time for me to grieve, I didn't do it. I was asked to take the funeral of my friend who died, and although I didn't want to take it, I did. I had to go back to my own church in Iowa and preach. I didn't want to preach because I was still in grief. It wasn't until about two or three weeks after the death that one of the associate pastors of our staff, Bob Parker, came over to my house, sat me down and said, "Ron, I want to read to you from the Bible. I want you to talk to me and I want to pray with you." When he did that I was able to get in touch with my grief. Now, for about two weeks I had been praying and the prayers would hit the ceiling and nothing was happening. I was screaming at God, "If you are there, why aren't you listening" and "What does all this mean?" but I was doing it all inside.

You have your problems and I have mine. I am working at expressing feelings now. But one of the ways in which my witness is inhibited is that I get so intensely into the work I do that I don't see that first of all I'm a person; secondly I am a pastor. We all have elements of Egypt in our personalities, but we dare not operate out of a theology of bondage if we are to declare the good news. Baptism has freed us from Egypt.

There are some on the other end of the spectrum who witness out of a second operative theology, a theology of glory. In effect they say, "I've got it, you need it, let me give it to you." Many, for example, don't see themselves in Egypt; they see themselves in the promised land. They believe that they have arrived. Some even call themselves sinless, though most would not take that position. It is possible to see by their works that they are involved in "triumphalism."

I've seen evidence of this at a practical level. Perhaps you have too. On a trip to a speaking engagement in North Dakota I was greeted in the Minneapolis airport by a young woman, a pretty young girl, who came up to me with a flower in her hand and a smile on her face and said, "Do you believe in God?" I had just gotten off the phone with a pastor friend who was going through a divorce. I was carrying a coat and two suitcases. I had a suitcase in each hand. I was on my way to the bathroom and I was in no mood for theological debate. Pinning a flower on me, she said, "Do you believe in God? Certainly you believe in God." I said, "Just a little." She said, "Well then you wouldn't mind making a contribution to God's cause, would you?" And I said, "Yes, I would mind. Thank you very much. Goodbye." She was caught in the trap of triumphalism.

There are many groups which do that kind of thing. It concerns me that people come at people in that way, not considering where they are but considering only the message they have to tell. Evangelism is thus done in a condescending way—"get with it," "do it now"—without any real reference to where the person is.

Gertrude Gillespie was the ugliest girl in town. Wes Seelinger tells the story of how she met a marvelous beautician by the name of Mr. J. Gertrude certainly never expected to meet him, though she heard of the reputation of Mr. J. He was supposed to have lived in the city, gone off to Paris, and learned how to be a great beautician. He could work marvels, she was told, but she never expected to meet him for she was poor. She couldn't afford to go to see him. One day the telephone rang. Gertrude Gillespie was a lonely woman and the telephone seldom rang. She answered it in haste. "This is Mr. J. I would like for you to come for an appointment."

"Oh," she said, "I can't do that. I don't have any money."

"No, this is free," said Mr. J. And so she went. From head to toe she was made into a new woman. When Mr. J. was all done that day Gertrude looked into the mirror. She couldn't believe what she saw. She thanked Mr. J. and off she went. As she approached people on the street she said, "My, you are ugly. Let me tell you about someone who can help you. Look what he has done for me." Then she got on the phone and called some of her associates and friends and said, "You know those blemishes you have? I know someone who can take care of them." Gertrude Gillespie started as a lonely, ugly woman. Gertrude Gillespie ended the same way. Her method of evangelizing is called triumphalism.

Historically we know there are evidences of triumphalism frequently connected with evangelism down through the ages. In the second century Montanus in Asia claimed he had the Holy Spirit and unless you were like him you weren't even a Christian; and he got a large following. Tertullian, an African church father of the third century, was a follower of Montanus. There was an urgency in these people to get out and bring others in because they had something which others needed.

We see evidences of the same kind of theology in the Roman Catholic church in religious and political forms in the imperialism of the Middle Ages. We see evidences of triumphalism in the

Schwärmerei of Luther's sixteenth-century Germany. These religious enthusiasts said, "We have it, you need it," and threw out all that in any way resembled Rome. Luther had more trouble with the *Schwärmerei* than he had with the Roman Catholic church. In our day Pentecostalism—much of it at least—has a sense of triumphalism frequently associated with the way it does evangelism.

Lutherans must not operate out of a theology of glory as we try to do evangelical outreach together.

"A Lutheran Context for Evangelism" necessitates that we look at the cross and the journey through the wilderness. Baptism has freed us from Egypt, so we are not in Egypt, but we are not yet in the promised land. We are moving toward it, but we are not yet there. We are a pilgrim people on the move; a people who offer bread to starving people. We Lutherans must get back to Luther, who saw the centrality of the cross for the people of God in the wilderness.

What is evangelism? It is one sinner saying to another sinner, one traveler saying to another traveler, one pilgrim saying to another pilgrim, "There's manna—I've seen it and I've tasted it and sometimes I've gotten tired of it and sometimes I've wanted something other than it, but it's God's food. It's there to be shared." How different that is from the wild forms of triumphalism or the mild forms of triumphalism which we've seen in history or in our day, with someone saying, "Are you saved, brother?" (implied: "I am"). "Have you been reborn?" (implied: "I have"). "Have you found it?" (implied: "I have found it!").

How different it is to be in the wilderness asking instead, "Where are you hurting? How are you feeling? What is it like to travel like you travel?" Those are better questions because they take seriously the fact that we are all traveling. I may know where the manna is. I may have seen a great light. I may have heard a great voice. I have known nuances of the Almighty, but I haven't seen God, for no one sees him and lives. "I have seen only his back parts," Moses said. "For no one sees God and lives. I haven't seen his front. I haven't seen his face. I've seen only his back parts." I don't know all that "back parts" means but I know it certainly means I've seen where God has been. I've seen the traces of God. I've seen the footsteps of God. I've looked back over my shoulder and I know that God is in my past. I may not have seen him in past events as they happened, but now that I think about it, his hand was certainly in my biography. I see his "back parts" but I don't see God, for this isn't the promised land. It is the wilderness. We're not *of* this wilderness, but we are *in* it.

The theology of glory is not a proper context for evangelism. The theology of the cross, a theology for the wilderness, is the context from which we speak. We Lutherans have too frequently spoken as if we had a different context, as if we were still in Egypt. This isn't Egypt. This is a time for following what light God has put before us.

The time is right. For Christ's sake, what are we doing? We don't have sight, but we have hope. We don't see perfectly. We see darkly like looking into a dim mirror. And what we see is very good, for it is an intimation of God that must be passed on. It must be shared.

In the marvelous third chapter of the Gospel of John, Jesus makes reference to Moses holding up the snake that those who were bitten and dying might look at it and live. Reference is then made to the cross yet coming . . . "So shall the Son of man be lifted up, and those who look shall live." That passage speaks of a theology for pilgrims who are sick and dying and sinful but who have a great God to whom they look, from whom they received power—a God who can be, who must be shared. Many are still back in Egypt and some who have started on the journey across the wilderness are tired and want to go home. They have mumbled and grumbled against God and said, "It's tough out here; it's easier back in Egypt." They need encouragement too, these lapsed members of your congregation and mine. They need time and effort and attention; most of all they need to look at the cross. The broken body of Jesus the carpenter on the cross is always the God before us, suffering before us in the wilderness. Think of it: God who goes before us—symbolized in a pillar of fire by night and a pillar of cloud by day—God is broken before we are even broken. God knows what it is to be where we are. Look at him; don't look at me, don't look at the church, look at him. There's a magnetic attraction in someone who goes that far. That's what's needed—a theology that looks at him.

People sometimes said to Harry Emerson Fosdick, "I don't believe in God." How do you deal with that question? Fosdick used to say, "Tell me about the God you don't believe in. Maybe I don't believe in him, either." The God that people don't believe in is generally not God but some figment of the imagination, some idol that has been created after our own image. The cross of Christ is the corrective for our illusions about God, so look up at the broken body of God on that Friday—that rainy Friday we've since called "good."

There's much more that might be said. I've simply tried to focus on evangelism, the heart of our gospel message. Evangelism is not the whole of our message but it is the heart of it. Evangelism is not in competition with liturgy, nor is it in competition with social action, nor is it in competition with anything except sin and the kind of personal bondages or illusions that capture us.

I've tried to focus on evangelism because there is so much that needs to be done and it now appears to be the *kairos*, the right time, God's time. It is time to look at the cross again.

Since that is so apparent to me I am made bold to conclude with a statement that I hope you will never forget. You will undoubtedly forget much of what I've said. A theological address is spoken and then gone. You won't even remember my name a few weeks or months from now. That isn't important anyway. I hope you'll hang onto this concluding statement: Because you are Christian; because you are baptized; because we have in front of us bold challenges to do evangelism together—to do it well and to do it out of love; because your leadership is needed in the Lutheran Church in America in Evangelical Outreach; because Jesus said, "Go with the good news to the world, witness for me"; but more, because evangelism will always be the heart of what we do; mostly because Jesus Christ is and will be with you always—"For Christ's sake, don't just sit there."